SUMMER BEFORE

GRADE 2

SUMMER LINK

MATH plus READING

Thinking Kids®
An imprint of Carson-Dellosa Publishing LLC
Greensboro, North Carolina

Thinking Kids®
An imprint of Carson-Dellosa Publishing LLC
P.O. Box 35665
Greensboro, NC 27425 USA

Printed in the USA • All rights reserved.   ISBN 978-1-4838-0465-1

09-105197784

Table of Contents
by Section

Summer Link Math
Table of Contents

Summer Link Reading
Table of Contents

This page intentionally left blank.

Summer LINK
MATH

Summer Link Super Edition Grade 2

Number Recognition 1, 2, 3, 4, 5

Directions: Use the color codes to color the parrot.

Color:
1's red
2's blue
3's yellow
4's green
5's orange

Number Recognition 6, 7, 8, 9, 10

Directions: Use the color codes to color the carousel horse.

Color:
6's purple
7's yellow
8's black
9's pink
10's brown

Numbers

Directions: Practice by tracing the words and numbers. Then write the words and numbers.

one 1

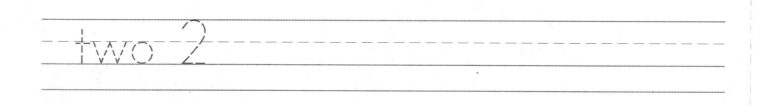

two 2

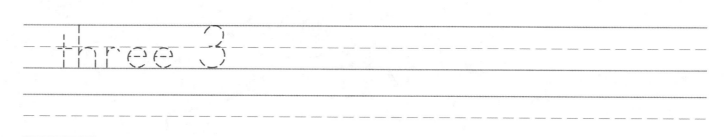

three 3

four 4

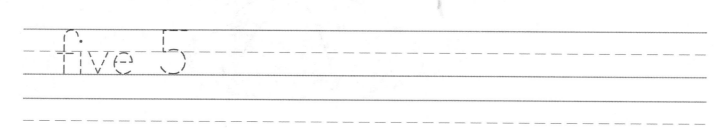

five 5

Numbers

Directions: Practice by tracing the words and numbers. Then write the words and numbers.

six 6

seven 7

eight 8

nine 9

ten 10

Numbers

Directions: Practice by tracing the words and numbers. Then write the words and numbers.

eleven 11

twelve 12

thirteen 13

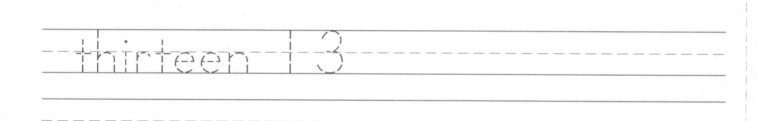

fourteen 14

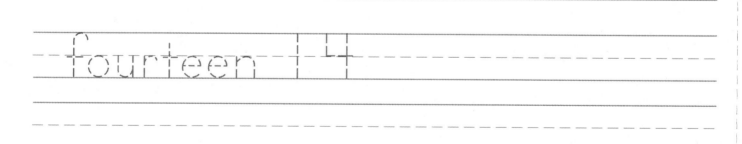

fifteen 15

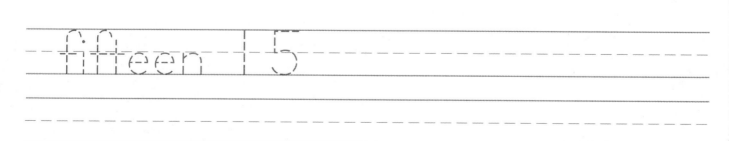

Numbers

Directions: Practice by tracing the words and numbers. Then write the words and numbers.

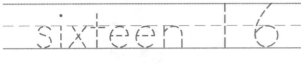

sixteen 16

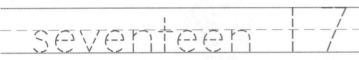

seventeen 17

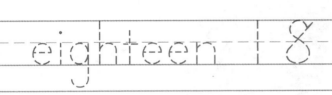

eighteen 18

nineteen 19

twenty 20

Shapes: Square

Directions: A **square** is a figure with four corners and four sides of the same length. This is a square: ☐ . Find the squares and draw a circle around them. Then, color the squares.

Directions: Trace the word. Then, write the word.

Shapes: Circle

Directions: A **circle** is a figure that is round. This is a circle:◯ . Find the circles and draw a square around them. Then, color the circles.

Directions: Trace the word. Then, write the word.

Shapes: Triangle

Directions: A **triangle** is a figure with three corners and three sides. This is a triangle: △ . Find the triangles and draw a circle around them. Then, color the triangles.

Directions: Trace the word. Then, write the word.

triangle

Name _____

Shapes: Rectangle

Directions: A **rectangle** is a figure with four corners and four sides. The sides opposite each other are the same length. This is a rectangle: ▭. Find the rectangles and draw a circle around them. Then, color the rectangles.

Directions: Trace the word. Then, write the word.

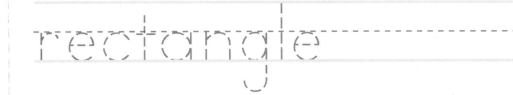

Shapes: Oval and Diamond

Directions: An **oval** is an egg-shaped figure. This is an oval: ⬭ .

A **diamond** is a figure with four sides. Its corners form points at the top, sides, and bottom. This is a diamond: ◇ .

Find the ovals. Color them red.
Find the diamond. Color it blue.

Directions: Trace the words. Then, write the words.

oval

diamond

Shapes: Review

Directions:
Trace the circles
Trace the squares
Trace the rectangles
Trace the triangles
Trace the ovals
Trace the diamonds

red
blue
yellow
green
purple
orange

Patterns: Shapes

Directions: Draw a line from the box on the left to the box on the right with the same shape and color pattern.

 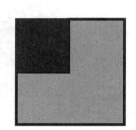  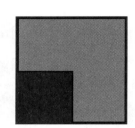

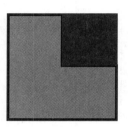   

   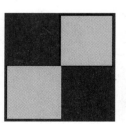

Patterns: Numbers

Mia likes to count by twos, threes, fours, fives, tens, and hundreds.

Directions: Complete the number patterns.

1. 5, ____, ____, 20, ____, ____, 35, ____, ____, 50

2. 100, ____, ____, 400, ____, ____, ____, 800, ____

3. ____, 4, 6, ____, ____, 12, ____, 16, ____, ____

4. 10, ____, ____, 40, ____, ____, 70, ____, 90

5. 4, ____, 12, ____, ____, 24, ____, 32, ____, 40

6. ____, 6, 9, ____, ____, 18, ____, 24, ____, 30

Directions: Make up two of your own number patterns.

____, ____, ____, ____, ____, ____, ____, ____

____, ____, ____, ____, ____, ____, ____, ____

Summer Link Super Edition Grade 2

Numbers: 0 – 10

Directions: Write the numeral for each number.

three ⭐⭐⭐ 3 _____   one  _____

five 🪀🪀🪀🪀🪀 _____   zero _____

two 🖍🖍 _____   six  _____

eight ⚫⚫⚫⚫⚫⚫⚫⚫ _____

ten △△△△△△△△△△ _____

nine ⬡⬡⬡⬡⬡⬡⬡⬡⬡ _____

seven ♥♥♥♥♥♥♥ _____

four ◼◼◼◼ _____

Directions: Tell how many dots.

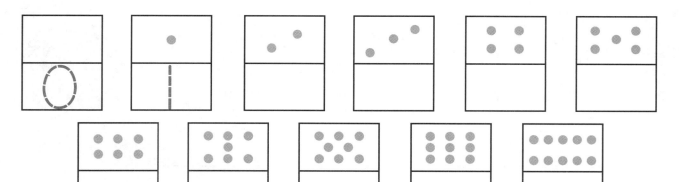

Numbers: Counting

Directions: Count each group of zoo animals. Draw a line from the number to the correct number word. The first one shows you what to do.

four

eight

one

ten

seven

six

two

three

nine

five

Numbers: Counting

Directions: Color the correct number of marbles in each bag.

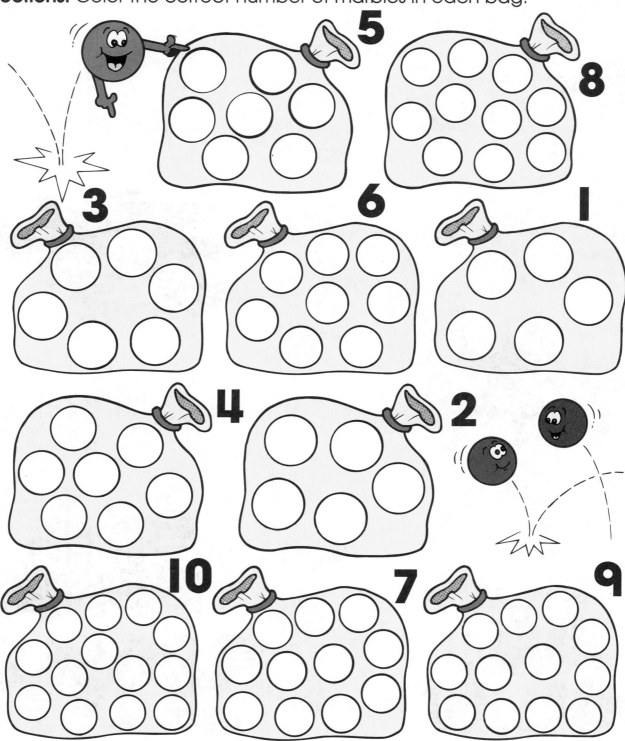

Name _____

Numbers: Counting

Directions: Read the clues to find out how many ears of corn each pig ate. Write the number on the line next to each pig.

I ate the number that comes before 26.

I ate the number that comes between 87 and 89.

I ate the number that comes after 92.

I ate the number that comes before 57.

I ate the number that comes between 39 and 41.

Patsy

Horace

Pinky

Hilda

Porky

Who ate the most?_____ Who ate the least?_____

Name _____

Counting: Twos, Fives, and Tens

Directions: Write the missing numbers.

Count by 2's.

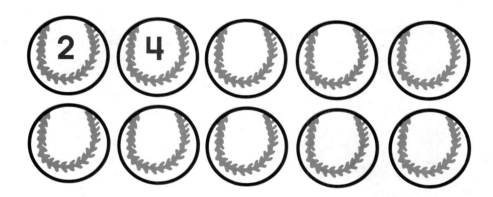

Count by 5's.

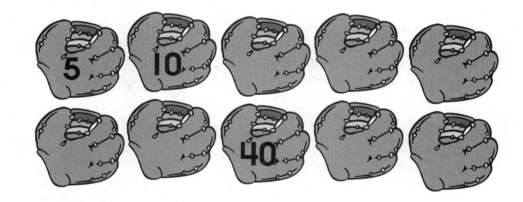

Count by 10's.

Name _____

Critter Count

Directions: Count by 2's, 5's, and 10's to find the "critter count."

Each worm = 2. Count by 2's to find the total.

 = _____

 = _____

Each turtle = 5. Count by 5's to find the total.

= _____

= _____

Each ladybug = 10. Count by 10's to find the total.

 = _____

 = _____

Counting: Fives

Directions: Count by fives to draw the path to the playground.

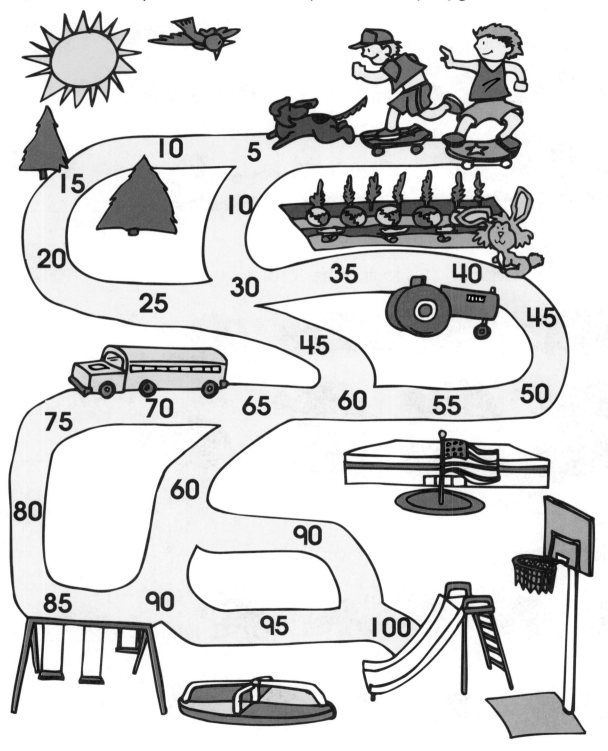

Counting: Tens

Directions: Count by 10's. Color each canteen with a 10 to lead the camel to the watering hole.

Summer Link Super Edition Grade 2

Counting: Tens

Directions: Count in order by tens to draw the path the boy takes to the store.

Addition: Creature Count

Directions: Add to find the sum. Write each answer on a spaceship.

$4 + 6 =$  10

$1 + 9 =$

$7 + 1 =$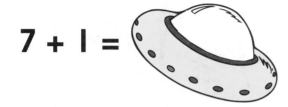

$7 + 3 =$

$5 + 2 =$

$6 + 1 =$

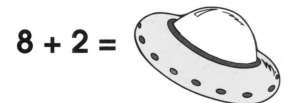

$8 + 2 =$

$3 + 5 =$

$6 + 3 =$

$6 + 2 =$

Summer Link Super Edition Grade 2

Name _____

Addition: Lumberjack Facts

Directions: Add to find the sum. Use the code to color the picture.

Code:
1 — red	3 — black	5 — brown
2 — yellow	4 — blue	6 — green

What is it? _____

Addition: Grid

Directions: Write the sums where the columns and rows meet. The first one shows you what to do.

+	1	2	3	4	5	6	7	8	9
1	2								
2									
3									
4									
5									
6									
7									
8									
9									

Addition: Math-Minded Mermaids

Directions: Look at each number. Then, look in each seashell. Circle each pair of numbers that can be added together to equal that number.

Addition: In the Doghouse

Directions: Look at the pictures. Complete the addition sentences.

2 + 6 =

7 + 3 =

6 + 1 =

4 + 5 =

6 + 2 =

7 + 2 =

Addition: Practice

Directions: Add.

6 +4	7 +2	4 +4	4 +5	9 +1	3 +2
2 +7	6 +2	9 +0	2 +5	1 +4	4 +6
8 +1	2 +2	3 +6	1 +7	7 +3	1 +8
2 +3	2 +8	3 +5	8 +2	6 +1	0 +9
1 +9	6 +3	3 +4	5 +2	5 +4	4 +3
5 +3	8 +0	5 +5	3 +7	2 +6	3 +3

Addition: Facts Through 12

Directions: Add.

2
+9
____
11

9
+2
____

3
+8
____

8
+3
____

5
+6
____

6
+5
____

4
+7
____

7
+4
____

8
+4
____

4
+8
____

7
+5
____

5
+7
____

9
+3
____

3
+9
____

6
+6
____

Directions: Add.

8
+3
____

6
+6
____

9
+3
____

3
+8
____

4
+7
____

2
+9
____

5
+7
____

8
+4
____

7
+5
____

5
+6
____

9
+2
____

4
+8
____

Subtraction: Secrets

Directions: Solve the subtraction problems. Use the code to find the secret message.

Code:

7	5	2	6	4	3
K	T	Y	E	W	A

PLEASE, DON'T EVER

8 -3	10 - 7	9 -2	10 - 4
___	___	___	___

9 -6	6 - 2	7 -4	8 -6
___	___	___	___

MY MATH!

Name _____

Subtraction: Facts Through 12

Directions: Subtract.

11 −9	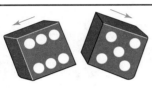	11 −2		11 −8	11 −3

11
−9

11
−2

11
−8

11
−3

11
−6

11
−5

11
−7

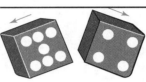

11
−4

12
−8

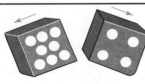

12
−4

12
−7

12
−5

12
−9

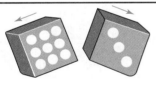

12
−3

12
−6

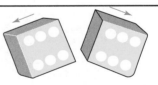

Subtract.

11   11   12   11   12   12
−3   −6   −3   −8   −7   −9

11   12   12   12   11   12
−7   −4   −5   −6   −2   −8

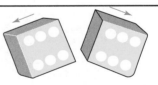

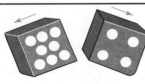
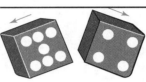

Subtraction: Practice

Directions: Subtract.

9 −4	7 −6	10 −5	9 −7	8 −5	10 −9
10 −4	6 −3	9 −6	10 −3	9 −0	5 −1
3 −1	9 −1	10 −8	7 −2	9 −5	2 −2
10 −1	7 −0	5 −3	8 −7	10 −2	6 −4
9 −8	7 −4	10 −0	4 −2	8 −4	9 −3
10 −6	8 −6	9 −2	8 −1	9 −9	10 −7

Addition and Subtraction

Directions: Solve the number problem under each picture. Write **+** or **−** to show if you should add or subtract.

How many  s in all?

7 + 5 = ____12____

How many  s in all?

8   3 = _____

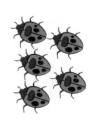

How many 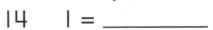 s are left?

9   4 = _____

How many 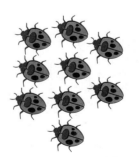 s are left?

14   1 = _____

How many  s in all?

15   6 = _____

How many s are left?

9   5 = _____

Addition and Subtraction

Directions: Add or subtract.
If you get 9, color the part red. If you get 14, color the part brown.

$$\begin{array}{r} 9 \\ -7 \\ \hline \end{array} \qquad \begin{array}{r} 3 \\ +4 \\ \hline \end{array} \qquad \begin{array}{r} 12 \\ -8 \\ \hline \end{array}$$

$$5 + 5 = \underline{\hspace{1cm}}$$

$$\begin{array}{r} 15 \\ -8 \\ \hline \end{array} \qquad \begin{array}{r} 7 \\ +5 \\ \hline \end{array} \qquad \begin{array}{r} 14 \\ -9 \\ \hline \end{array}$$

$$11 - 7 = \underline{\hspace{1cm}}$$

$$14 - 5 = \underline{\hspace{1cm}}$$

$$7 - 6 = \underline{\hspace{1cm}}$$

$$\begin{array}{r} 8 \\ +6 \\ \hline \end{array} \qquad \begin{array}{r} 6 \\ -5 \\ \hline \end{array}$$

$$\begin{array}{r} 18 \\ -9 \\ \hline \end{array} \qquad \begin{array}{r} 11 \\ -3 \\ \hline \end{array} \qquad \begin{array}{r} 6 \\ +3 \\ \hline \end{array}$$

$$4 + 8 = \underline{\hspace{1cm}}$$

$$\begin{array}{r} 13 \\ -4 \\ \hline \end{array} \qquad \begin{array}{r} 2 \\ +7 \\ \hline \end{array} \qquad \begin{array}{r} 17 \\ -8 \\ \hline \end{array}$$

$$\begin{array}{r} 4 \\ +5 \\ \hline \end{array} \qquad \begin{array}{r} 16 \\ -7 \\ \hline \end{array} \qquad \begin{array}{r} 12 \\ -3 \\ \hline \end{array} \qquad \begin{array}{r} 15 \\ -6 \\ \hline \end{array} \qquad \begin{array}{r} 13 \\ -8 \\ \hline \end{array}$$

$$\begin{array}{r} 5 \\ +9 \\ \hline \end{array}$$

$$\begin{array}{r} 6 \\ +8 \\ \hline \end{array}$$

$$\begin{array}{r} 5 \\ +6 \\ \hline \end{array} \qquad \begin{array}{r} 10 \\ -7 \\ \hline \end{array} \qquad \begin{array}{r} 6 \\ +6 \\ \hline \end{array} \qquad \begin{array}{r} 8 \\ +9 \\ \hline \end{array} \qquad \begin{array}{r} 11 \\ -5 \\ \hline \end{array} \qquad \begin{array}{r} 9 \\ +7 \\ \hline \end{array} \qquad \begin{array}{r} 8 \\ +8 \\ \hline \end{array}$$

$$\begin{array}{r} 7 \\ +7 \\ \hline \end{array} \qquad \begin{array}{r} 9 \\ +5 \\ \hline \end{array}$$

Addition and Subtraction

Directions:

Add.

5 +4 9	4 +3	1 +2	5 +3	4 +6	4 +4
0 +6	4 +1	8 +1	9 +1	8 +2	2 +2
2 +7	5 +2	1 +6	5 +5	4 +5	6 +2

Subtract.

10 −6 4	8 −2	5 −3	7 −6	4 −3	10 −5
9 −3	10 −2	7 −2	8 −6	10 −9	8 −8
10 −4	9 −6	9 −8	8 −1	10 −7	7 −4

Addition: Review

Directions: Add.

```
  24        75        50        62        46
 +13       + 4       +27       +15       +23
  37        79
```

```
  52        96        73        38        35
 +34       + 2       +16       +40       +21
```

```
  10        14        12        33        13
 +21       + 5       +34       +53       +11
```

```
  24        57        60        12        71
 +21       + 2       +33       +43       +26
```

```
  16        28        51        40        63
 +52       + 1       +27       +45       +16
```

```
  22        64        24        41        31
 +67       + 4       +72       +38       +56
```

Subtraction: Review

Directions: Subtract.

75 −34 41	67 − 4 63	30 −20	48 −30	55 −32
78 −67	56 − 3	98 −86	86 −15	98 −48
95 −31	84 − 2	65 −45	79 −48	84 −50
42 −10	39 − 6	89 −42	67 −21	66 −36
98 −73	72 − 2	43 −13	57 −32	69 −15
32 −11	97 − 5	78 −22	99 −16	87 −47

Place Value: Tens and Ones

The place value of a digit, or numeral, is shown by where it is in the number. For example, in the number **23, 2** has the place value of **tens**, and **3** is **ones**.

Directions: Count the groups of ten crayons and write the number by the word **tens**. Count the other crayons and write the number by the word **ones**.

Example: + = __|__ ten + __|__ one

 = ____ tens + ____ ones

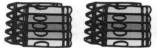  + = ____ tens + ____ ones

 = ____ tens + ____ ones

---

6 tens + 3 ones = ____   5 tens + 1 one = ____

3 tens + 8 ones = ____   9 tens + 7 ones = ____

4 tens + 5 ones = ____   2 tens + 8 ones = ____

Name _____

Place Value: Ones, Tens

Directions: Write the numbers for the tens and ones. Then add.

Example:

2 tens + 7 ones

20 + 7

27

6 tens + 2 ones

___ + ___

___

3 tens + 4 ones

___ + ___

___

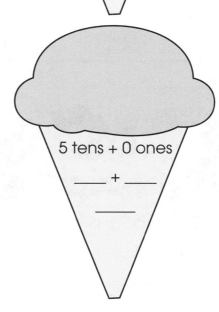

8 tens + 3 ones

___ + ___

___

5 tens + 0 ones

___ + ___

___

Place Value: Hundreds

Directions: Write the numbers for hundreds, tens, and ones. Then add.

Example:

1 hundred + 4 tens + 6 ones
100 + 40 + 6
146

7 hundreds + 3 tens + 5 ones
_____ + _____ + _____
_____

3 hundreds + 1 ten + 9 ones
_____ + _____ + _____
_____

5 hundreds + 8 tens + 0 ones
_____ + _____ + _____
_____

9 hundreds + 0 tens + 7 ones
_____ + _____ + _____
_____

Name _____

Fractions: Whole and Half

A fraction is a number that names part of a whole, such as $\frac{1}{2}$ or $\frac{3}{4}$.

Directions: Color half of each object.

Example:

Whole apple

Half an apple

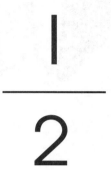

$$\frac{1}{2}$$

Fractions: Halves $\frac{1}{2}$

$\frac{1}{2}$ $\frac{\text{Part shaded or divided}}{\text{Number of equal parts}}$

Directions: Color only the shapes that show halves.

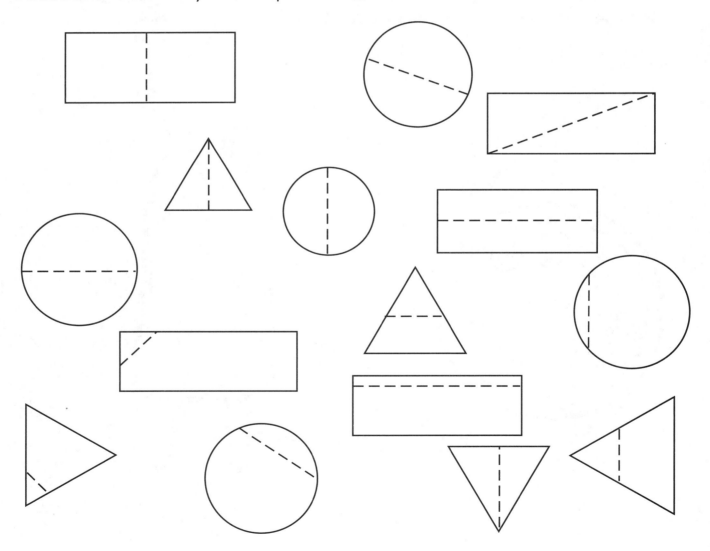

Fractions: Thirds $\frac{1}{3}$

Directions: Circle the objects that have 3 equal parts.

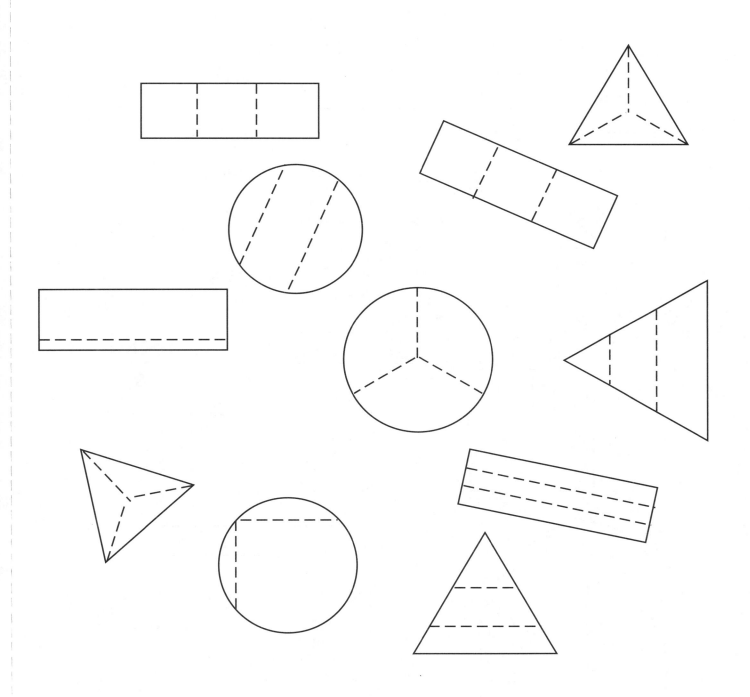

Fractions: Fourths $\frac{1}{4}$

Directions: Circle the objects that have 4 equal parts.

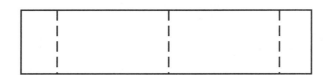

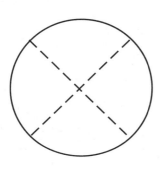
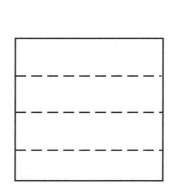
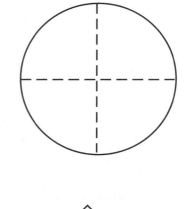

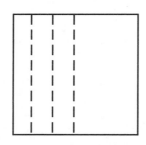
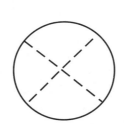
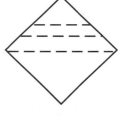

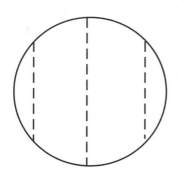
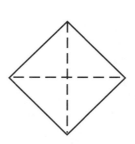
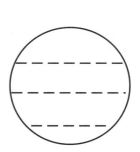

Fractions: Thirds and Fourths

Directions: Each object has 3 equal parts. Color one section.

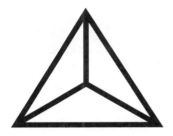

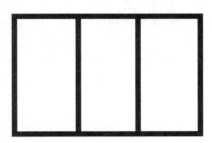

Directions: Each object has 4 equal parts. Color one section.

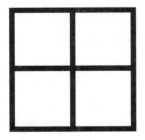

Name _____

Fractions: Review

How many equal parts?

 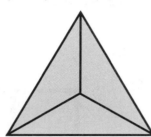 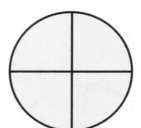 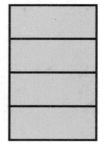 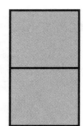

2 _____ _____ _____ _____

Directions: Color shapes with 2 equal parts red. Color shapes with 3 equal parts blue. Color shapes with 4 equal parts green.

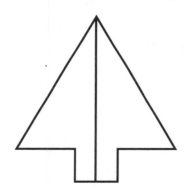 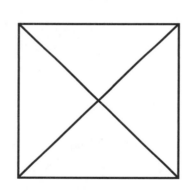 

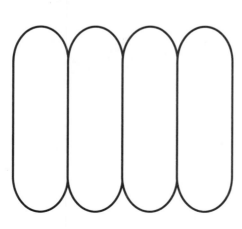 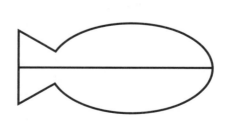 

Fractions: Review

Directions: Count the equal parts, then write the fraction.

Example:

Shaded part = ___1___

Equal parts = ___3___

Write $\frac{1}{3}$

Shaded part = ___1___

Equal parts = _____

Write _____

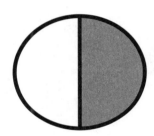

Shaded part = ___1___

Equal parts = _____

Write _____

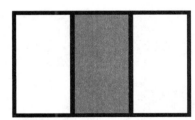

Shaded part = ___1___

Equal parts = _____

Write _____

Money: Counting Pennies

A **penny** is worth 1¢.

Directions: Count the money. Write how much.

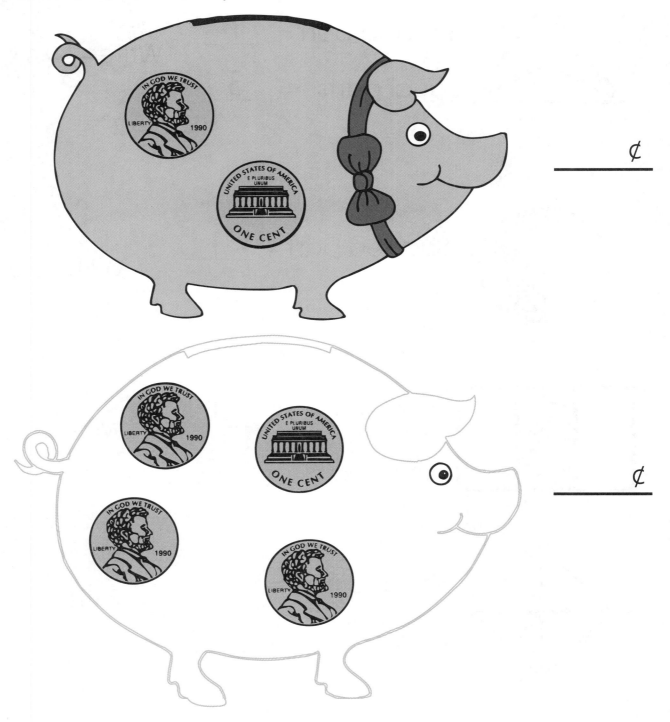

_____ ¢

_____ ¢

Money: Counting Pennies

Who has more money?

Directions: Count the money.
Write the amount.

_____ ¢

_____ ¢

Directions: Circle the answer.
Who has more money?

Name _____

Money: Counting With Nickels and Pennies

Directions: Count the coins on each "**cent**"-ipede.

_____ ¢

_____ ¢

_____ ¢

_____ ¢

_____ ¢

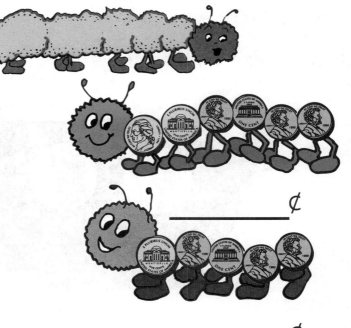

_____ ¢

_____ ¢

_____ ¢

_____ ¢

Money: Nickels

Directions: Count the nickels. Write the amount of money in each meter.

Example:

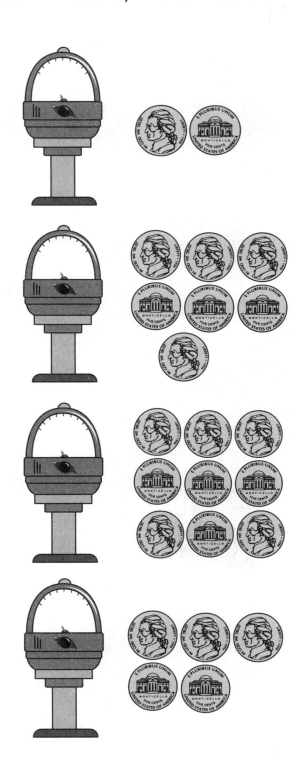

Name _____

Money: Penny, Nickel, Dime

Directions: Draw a line from the toy to the amount of money it costs.

Name _____

Money: Penny, Nickel, Dime

  I penny 1¢

  I nickel 5¢

  I dime 10¢

Directions: Tell how much money.

_____ ¢

_____ ¢

_____ ¢

_____ ¢

_____ ¢

_____ ¢

_____ ¢

_____ ¢

61

Name _____

Money: Penny, Nickel, Dime

Directions: Count the money on each belt. Write the amount under the belt.

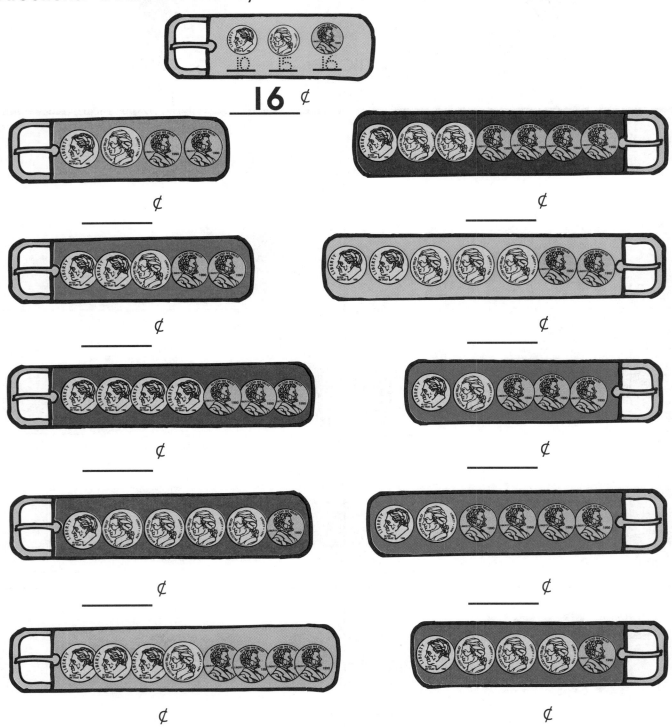

16 ¢

_____ ¢

_____ ¢

_____ ¢

_____ ¢

_____ ¢

_____ ¢

_____ ¢

_____ ¢

_____ ¢

_____ ¢

Name _____

Money: Quarters

Directions: It costs 25¢ to catch a fish. Circle each group of coins that makes 25¢. How many fish can I catch?

Directions: Draw and color the fish I can catch.

Money: Quarters

Some children had fun spending the allowance they earned. The boys bought some cars.

Terry paid 5¢ for each **blue** car.
Directions: Color Terry's cars **blue**.

How much did Terry pay for the **blue** cars?

 _____ ¢

Lucas liked the **red** cars. They were the same price.
Color his cars **red**.

How much did Lucas pay for the **red** cars?

_____ ¢

Which boy paid more? _____

Money: Problem Solving

Directions: Add or subtract.

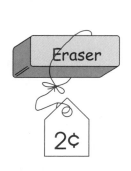 Eraser 2¢

 4¢

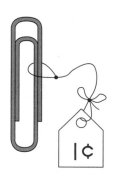 1¢

 CRAYON 3¢

I buy   1 ¢

I buy CRAYON   + 3 ¢

I spend   4 ¢

I buy   ¢

I buy   + ¢

I spend   ¢

I buy Eraser   ¢

I buy    + ¢

I spend   ¢

I buy CRAYON   ¢

I buy Eraser   + ¢

I spend   ¢

I have    5 ¢

I buy CRAYON   − 3 ¢

I have left   ¢

I have   ¢

I buy   − ¢

I have left   ¢

Time: Hour

The short hand of the clock tells the hour. The long hand tells how many minutes after the hour. When the minute hand is on the **12**, it is the beginning of the hour.

Directions: Look at each clock. Write the time.

Example:

___3__ o'clock

____ o'clock

____ o'clock

____ o'clock

____ o'clock

____ o'clock

____ o'clock

____ o'clock

____ o'clock

Time: Hour

Directions: Color the little hour hand **red**.
Fill in the blanks.

The BIG HAND is on _____.
The little hand is on _____.

It is _____ o'clock.

The BIG HAND is on _____.
The little hand is on _____.

It is _____ o'clock.

The BIG HAND is on _____.
The little hand is on _____.

It is _____ o'clock.

The BIG HAND is on _____.
The little hand is on _____.

It is _____ o'clock.

Time: Practice

Directions: What is the time? Write the answers below.

_____ o'clock   _____ o'clock   _____ o'clock

_____ o'clock   _____ o'clock   _____ o'clock

_____ o'clock   _____ o'clock   _____ o'clock

_____ o'clock   _____ o'clock

Name _____

Time: Poems

Directions: Read each poem. Draw a line to the clock that matches.

It is 2 o'clock.
Now it is dark night.
I am in bed,
All tucked in tight.

It is 12 o'clock,
And time to eat.
Have a sandwich,
Then a treat!

It is 5 o'clock.
Night is almost here.
Evening shadows
Are very near.

Time: Hour

4:00

4 o'clock
4:00

Both clocks show the same time.

Directions: Write the time for each clock.

|  |  |

o'clock

___1___

___1___ : ___OO___

o'clock

_____

_____ : ___OO___

o'clock

_____

_____ : ___OO___

4:00

o'clock

_____

_____ : _____

5:00

o'clock

_____

_____ : _____

6:00

o'clock

_____

_____ : _____

o'clock

_____

_____ : _____

o'clock

_____

_____ : _____

o'clock

_____

_____ : _____

Time: Hour

Directions: Circle the little hour hand on each clock. Write the time below.

_____ o'clock

_____ o'clock

_____ o'clock

_____ o'clock

_____ o'clock

_____ o'clock

Name _____

Time: Hour, Half-Hour

An hour is sixty minutes. The short hand of a clock tells the hour. It is written **0:00**, such as **5:00**. A half-hour is thirty minutes. When the long hand of the clock is pointing to the **6**, the time is on the half-hour. It is written **:30**, such as **5:30**.

Directions: Study the examples.
Tell what time it is on each clock.

Examples:

 **9:00** _____

The minute hand is on the 12.
The hour hand is on the 9.
It is 9 o'clock.

 **4:30** _____

The minute hand is on the 6.
The hour hand is between
the 4 and 5. It is 4:30.

_____ _____ _____ _____ _____

_____ _____ _____ _____ _____

Time: Hour, Half-Hour

The short hand of a clock tells the hour. The long hand tells how many minutes after the hour. When the minute hand is on the **6**, it is on the half-hour. A half-hour is thirty minutes. It is written **:30**, such as **5:30**.

Directions: Look at each clock. Write the time.

Example:

hour   half-hour

__1__ : __30__

____ : ____   ____ : ____   ____ : ____   ____ : ____

____ : ____   ____ : ____   ____ : ____   ____ : ____

Name _____

Time: Half-Hour

I o'clock
1:00

one thirty
1:30

2 o'clock
2:00

Directions: Write the time for each clock.

two _____ thirty

2 : 30

_____ thirty

_____ : 30

_____ thirty

_____ : 30

11:30

_____ thirty

_____ : _____

12:30

_____ thirty

_____ : _____

5:30

_____ thirty

_____ : _____

_____ thirty

_____ : _____

_____ thirty

_____ : _____

_____ thirty

_____ : _____

Time: Half-Hour

Directions: What time is it? Write the times below.

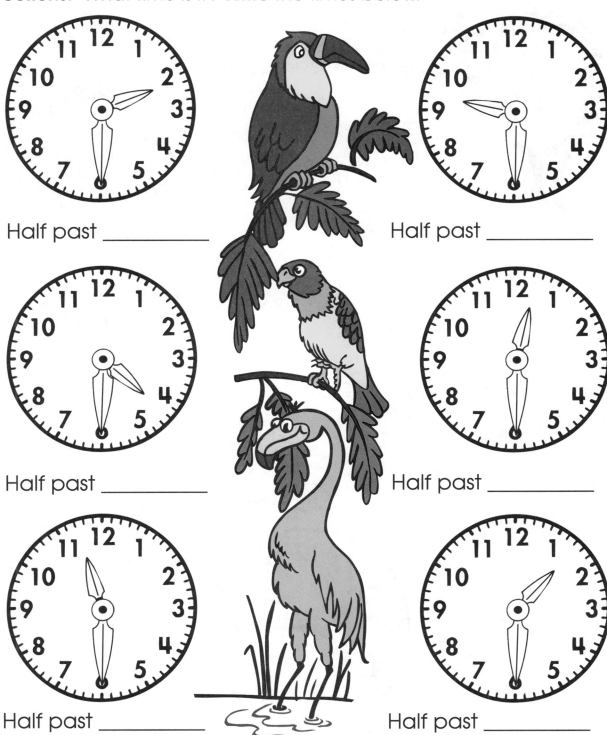

Half past _____

Half past _____

Half past _____

Half past _____

Half past _____

Half past _____

Time: Introduction to the Quarter-Hour

Each **hour** has **60** minutes.

An **hour** has **4** quarter-hours.

A **quarter-hour** is **15** minutes.

This clock face shows a quarter of an hour.

From the 12 to the 3 is 15 minutes.

From the 12 to the 3 is 15 minutes.

___15___ minutes after ___8___ o'clock

is ___8:15___

Time: Telling Time

Can you speak "clock time?"

1. "Quarter after" means 15 minutes after the hour.
2. "Half past" means 30 minutes after the hour.
3. "Quarter to" means 15 minutes until the next hour.

Directions: Write the quarter-hours from this time.

__8__ o'clock

quarter past _____

half past _____

quarter to _____

next hour: _____ o'clock

Time: Counting by Fives

Directions: Fill in the numbers on the clock face. Count by fives around the clock.

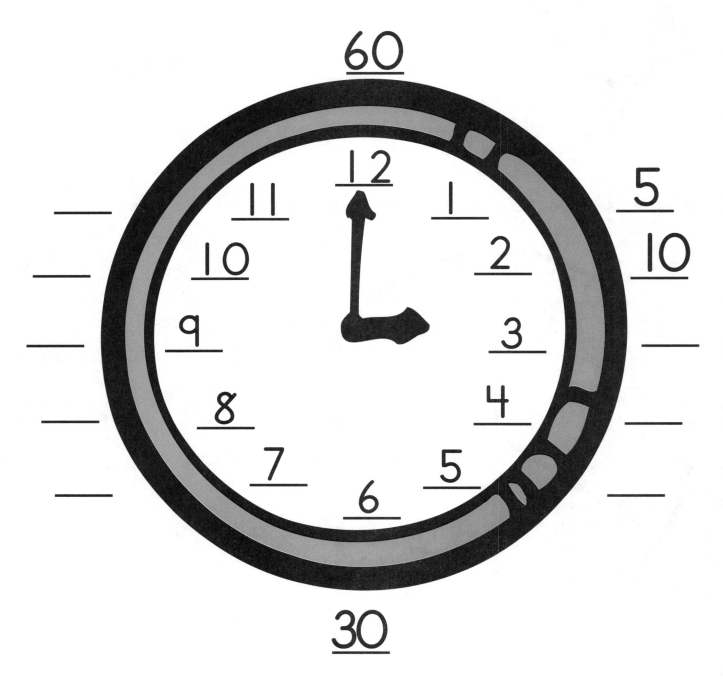

There are ___ minutes in one hour.

Time: Introduction to the Minute Intervals

Each number on the clock face stands for 5 minutes.

Directions: Count by 5's beginning at 12.
Write the numbers here:

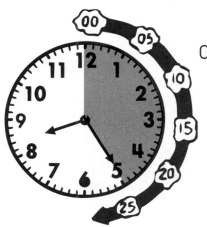

00 _05_ _10_ _15_ _20_ _25_

It is _25_ minutes after _8_ o'clock.

It is written 8:25.

Count by 5's.

00 ____ ____ ____ ____ ____ ____

It is ____ minutes after ____ o'clock.

____ : ____

Time: Introduction to the Minute Intervals

Directions: Write the time both ways.

00 05 10

10 minutes after 8 o'clock

8 : 10

00 ____ ____ ____ ____

____ minutes after ____ o'clock

____ : ____

00 ____ ____ ____ ____ ____ ____

____ ____

____ minutes after ____ o'clock

____ : ____

00 ____ ____ ____ ____ ____ ____

____ ____ ____ ____ ____

____ minutes after ____ o'clock

____ : ____

Circle the clocks with times between 3 o'clock and 9 o'clock.

Name _____

Time: Calendar

September						
S	M	T	W	Th	F	S
	1	2	3	4	5	6
7	8	9	10	11	12	13
14	15	16	17	18	19	20
21	22	23	24	25	26	27
28	29	30				

There are 12 months in a year.

September has exactly 30 days.

September 1 is on Monday.

There are 5 Mondays in September.

There are 4 Saturdays in September.

September 19 is on _____ .

Directions: Complete.

How many days are in a week? _____ .

What day comes after Thursday? _____ .

September 30 is on _____ .

There are _____ Tuesdays in September.

Days of the Week
Sunday
Monday
Tuesday
Wednesday
Thursday
Friday
Saturday

October						
S	M	T	W	Th	F	S
			1	2	3	4
5	6	7	8	9	10	11
12	13	14	15	16	17	18
19	20	21	22	23	24	25
26	27	28	29	30	31	

October has exactly _____ days.

October 1 is on _____ .

There are _____ Wednesdays in October.

October 31 is on _____ .

There are _____ Sundays in October.

Time: Calendar

March	Our Weather Calendar					
Sun.	Mon	Tues.	Wed	Thurs.	Fri.	Sat.
				1	2	3
4	5	6	7	8	9	10
11	12	13	14	15	16	17
18	19	20	21	22	23	24
25	26	27	28	29	30	31

sunny

rainy

cloudy

snowy

stormy

Directions: Complete.

What was the weather on

March 4? _____   March 10? _____

March 15? _____   March 21? _____

March 30? _____   March 31? _____

How many days did it rain  ?   _____

How many days did it storm ? _____

How many days did it snow ? _____

How many days was it cloudy ? _____

How many days was it sunny ? _____

Graphs

A graph is a drawing that shows information about numbers.

Directions: Count the apples in each row. Color the boxes to show how many apples have bites taken out of them.

Example:

83   **Summer Link Super Edition Grade 2**

Graphs

Directions: Count the fish. Color the bowls to make a graph that shows the number of fish.

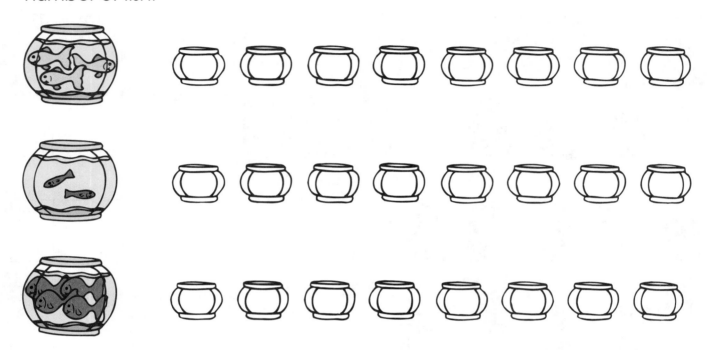

Directions: Use your fishbowl graphs to find the answers to the following questions. Draw a line to the correct bowl.

The most fish

The fewest fish

Greater Than, Less Than

Directions: In each shape, circle the smallest number. Draw a square around the largest number.

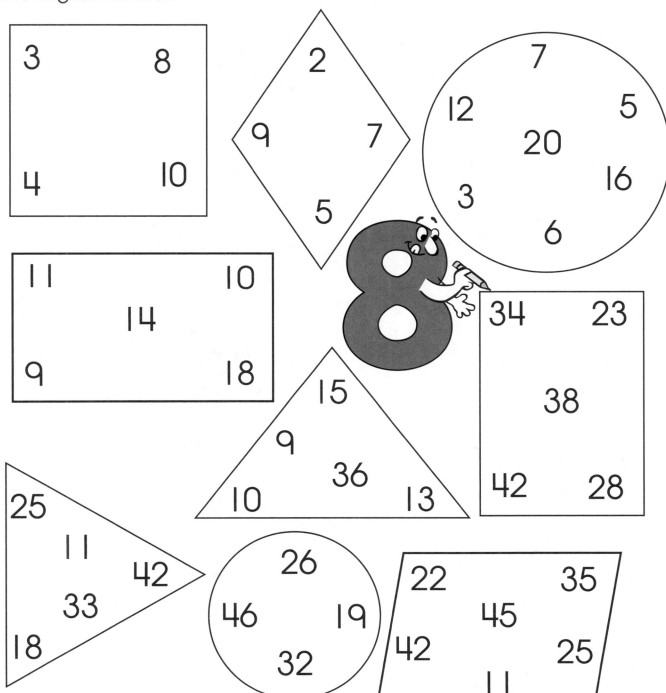

Summer Link Super Edition Grade 2

Name _____

Greater Than, Less Than

Directions: The open mouth points to the larger number. The small point goes to the smaller number. Draw the symbol < or > to the correct number.

Example: 5 $>$ 3

This means that 5 is greater than 3, and 3 is less than 5.

12 $\bigcirc$ 2   16 $\bigcirc$ 6

16 $\bigcirc$ 15   1 $\bigcirc$ 2

7 $\bigcirc$ 1   19 $\bigcirc$ 5

9 $\bigcirc$ 6   11 $\bigcirc$ 13

Greater Than, Less Than

Directions: Write < or > in each circle. Make sure the "mouth" is open toward the greater number.

26 ◯ 39

25 ◯ 43

10 ◯ 8

64 ◯ 11

43 ◯ 66

58 ◯ 70

19 ◯ 16

35 ◯ 9

80 ◯ 79

60 ◯ 57

Measurement: The Inch Worm

Directions: Use an inch ruler to measure these worms to the nearest inch.

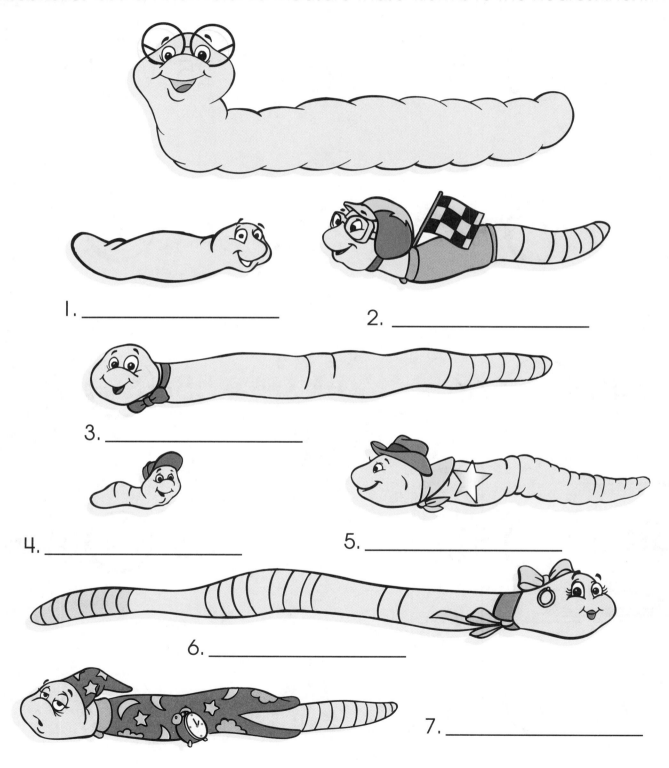

1. _____

2. _____

3. _____

4. _____

5. _____

6. _____

7. _____

Measurement: Inches

An **inch** is a unit of length in the standard measurement system.

Directions: Use a ruler to measure each object to the nearest inch.

I inch

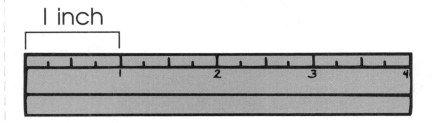

about _____ inches

about _____ inches

about _____ inches

about _____ inches

about _____ inches

about _____ inches

about _____ inches

Measurement: Inches

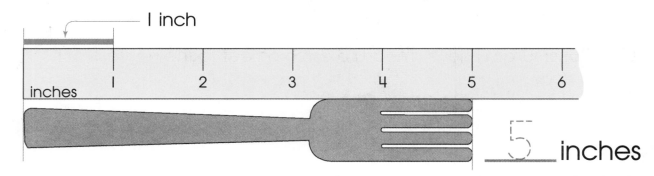

I inch

inches   1   2   3   4   5   6

___5___ inches

Directions: How long is each object?

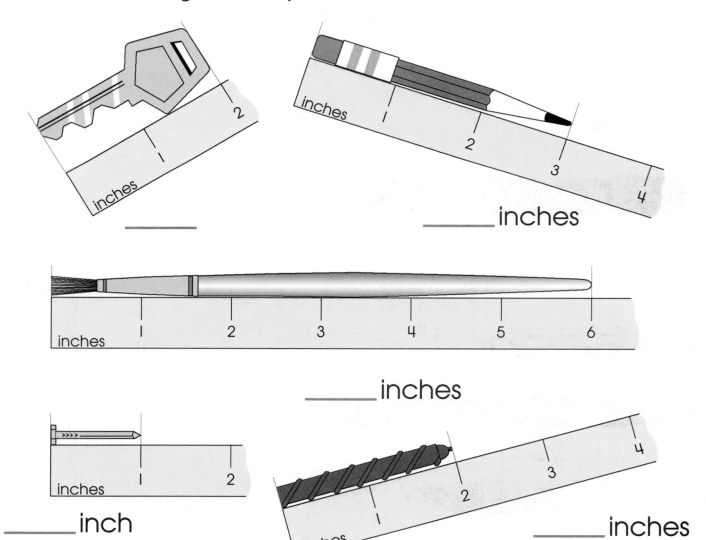

_____

_____ inches

_____ inches

_____ inch

_____ inches

Measurement: Measuring

Directions: Work with a friend.
Use a centimeter ruler. Measure each other.

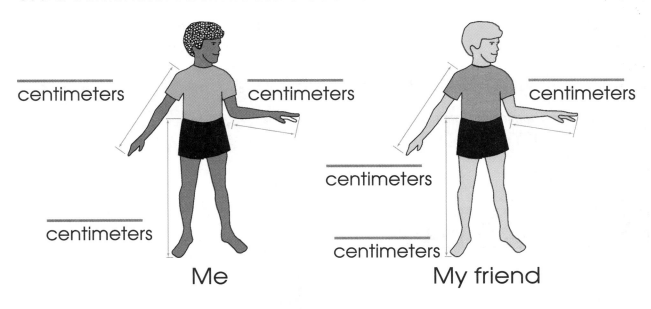

_____ centimeters

_____ centimeters

_____ centimeters

Me

_____ centimeters

_____ centimeters

_____ centimeters

My friend

Directions: Use an inch ruler.
Measure each other.

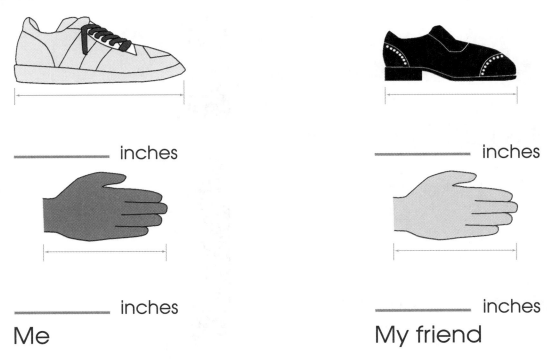

_____ inches

_____ inches

Me

_____ inches

_____ inches

My friend

Measurement: Centimeters

A **centimeter** is a unit of length in the metric system. There are 2.54 centimeters in an inch.

Directions: Use a centimeter ruler to measure the crayons to the nearest centimeter.

Example: The first crayon is about 7 centimeters long.

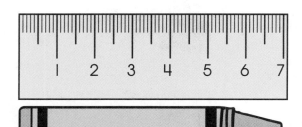

about ___7___ centimeters

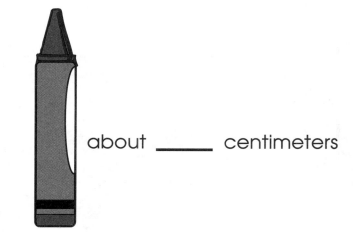

about _____ centimeters

about _____ centimeter

about _____ centimeters

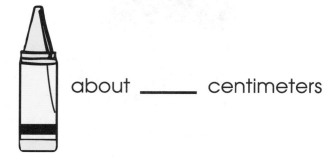

about _____ centimeters

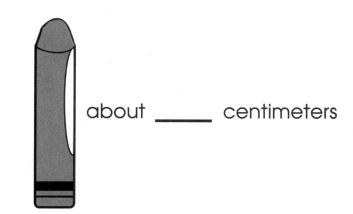

about _____ centimeters

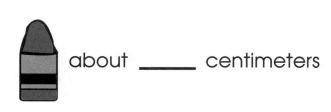

about _____ centimeters

Name _____

Measurement: Centimeters

Directions: The giraffe is about 8 centimeters high. How many centimeters (cm) high are the trees? Write your answers in the blanks.

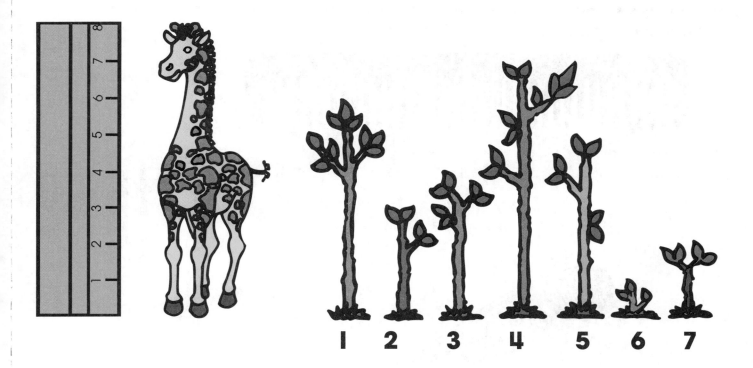

1. _____cm   2. _____cm   3. _____cm   4. _____cm

5. _____cm   6. _____cm   7. _____cm

93   Summer Link Super Edition Grade 2

Measurement: Centimeters

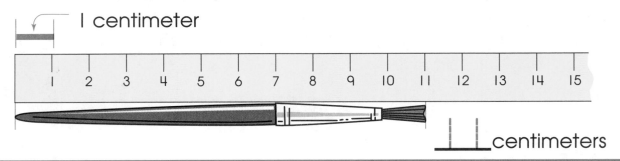

I centimeter

| 1 | 2 | 3 | 4 | 5 | 6 | 7 | 8 | 9 | 10 | 11 | 12 | 13 | 14 | 15 |

____ centimeters

Directions: How long is each object?

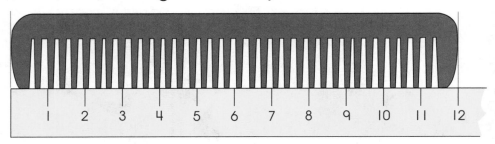

____ centimeters

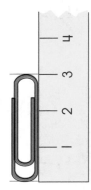

____ centimeters

____ centimeters

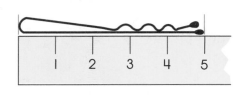

____ centimeters

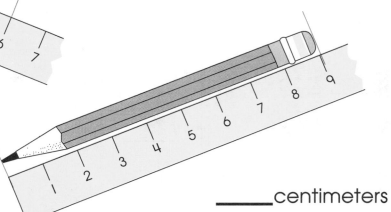

____ centimeters

Page 14

Shapes: Square

Directions: A **square** is a figure with four corners and four sides of the same length. This is a square: ☐. Find the squares and draw a circle around them. Then, color the squares.

Directions: Trace the word. Then, write the word.

square   square

Page 15

Shapes: Circle

Directions: A **circle** is a figure that is round. This is a circle: ◯. Find the circles and draw a square around them. Then, color the circles.

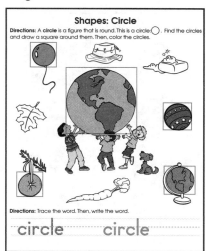

Directions: Trace the word. Then, write the word.

circle   circle

Page 16

Shapes: Triangle

Directions: A **triangle** is a figure with three corners and three sides. This is a triangle: △. Find the triangles and draw a circle around them. Then, color the triangles.

Directions: Trace the word. Then, write the word.

triangle   triangle

Page 17

Shapes: Rectangle

Directions: A **rectangle** is a figure with four corners and four sides. The sides opposite each other are the same length. This is a rectangle: ▭. Find the rectangles and draw a circle around them. Then, color the rectangles.

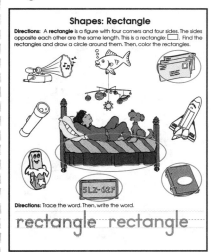

Directions: Trace the word. Then, write the word.

rectangle   rectangle

Page 18

Shapes: Oval and Diamond

Directions: An **oval** is an egg-shaped figure. This is an oval: ◯.

A **diamond** is a figure with four sides. Its corners form points at the top, sides, and bottom. This is a diamond: ◇.

Find the ovals. Color them red.
Find the diamond. Color it blue.

Directions: Trace the words. Then, write the words.

oval   oval
diamond   diamond

Page 19

Shapes: Review

Directions: Trace the circles   red
Trace the squares   blue
Trace the rectangles   yellow
Trace the triangles   green
Trace the ovals   purple
Trace the diamonds   orange

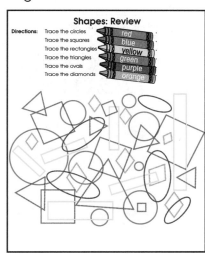

Page 20

Patterns: Shapes

Directions: Draw a line from the box on the left to the box on the right with the same shape and color pattern.

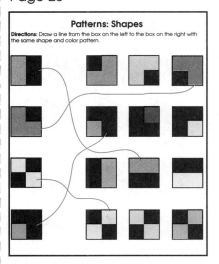

Page 21

Patterns: Numbers

Mia likes to count by twos, threes, fours, fives, tens, and hundreds.

Directions: Complete the number patterns.

1. 5, _10_, _15_, 20, _25_, _30_, 35, _40_, _45_, 50

2. 100, _200_, _300_, 400, _500_, _600_, _700_, 800, _900_

3. _2_, 4, 6, _8_, _10_, 12, _14_, 16, _18_, _20_

4. 10, _20_, _30_, 40, _50_, _60_, 70, _80_, 90

5. 4, _8_, 12, _16_, _20_, 24, _28_, 32, _36_, 40

6. _3_, 6, 9, _12_, _15_, 18, _21_, 24, _27_, 30

Directions: Make up two of your own number patterns.

____, ____, ____, ____, ____

Answers will vary.

____, ____, ____, ____, ____

Page 22

Numbers: 0 – 10

Directions: Write the numeral for each number.

three ☆☆☆ _3_   one ⊚ _1_

five 🐚🐚🐚🐚🐚 _5_   zero _0_

two ✏✏ _2_   six ‖‖‖‖‖‖ _6_

eight ●●●●●●●● _8_

ten △△△△△△△△△△ _10_

nine ⬢⬢⬢⬢⬢⬢⬢⬢⬢ _9_

seven ♥♥♥♥♥♥♥ _7_

four ▯▯▯▯ _4_

Directions: Tell how many dots.

0	1	2	3	4	5
6	7	8	9	10	

Page 23

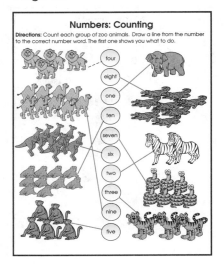

Numbers: Counting

Directions: Count each group of zoo animals. Draw a line from the number to the correct number word. The first one shows you what to do.

four
eight
one
ten
seven
six
two
three
nine
five

Page 24

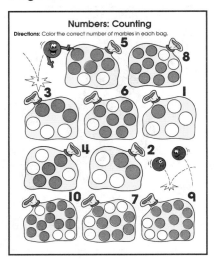

Numbers: Counting

Directions: Color the correct number of marbles in each bag.

5
8
3
6
1
4
2
10
7
9

Page 25

Numbers: Counting

Directions: Read the clues to find out how many ears of corn each pig ate. Write the number on the line next to each pig.

Patsy — I ate the number that comes before 26. — 25

Horace — I ate the number that comes between 87 and 89. — 88

Pinky — I ate the number that comes after 92. — 93

Hilda — I ate the number that comes before 57. — 56

Porky — I ate the number that comes between 39 and 41. — 40

Who ate the most? __Pinky__   Who ate the least? __Patsy__

Page 26

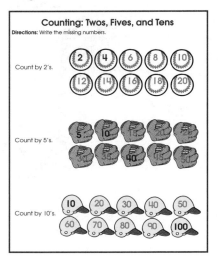

Counting: Twos, Fives, and Tens

Directions: Write the missing numbers.

Count by 2's. 2 4 6 8 10 12 14 16 18 20

Count by 5's. 5 10 15 20 25 30 35 40 45 50

Count by 10's. 10 20 30 40 50 60 70 80 90 100

Page 27

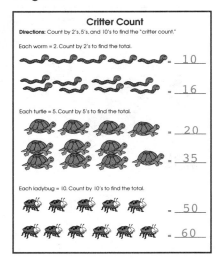

Critter Count

Directions: Count by 2's, 5's, and 10's to find the "critter count."

Each worm = 2. Count by 2's to find the total.

= 10
= 16

Each turtle = 5. Count by 5's to find the total.

= 20
= 35

Each ladybug = 10. Count by 10's to find the total.

= 50
= 60

Page 28

Counting: Fives

Directions: Count by fives to draw the path to the playground.

Page 29

Counting: Tens

Directions: Count by 10's. Color each canteen with a 10 to lead the camel to the watering hole.

Page 30

Counting: Tens

Directions: Count in order by tens to draw the path the boy takes to the store.

Page 31

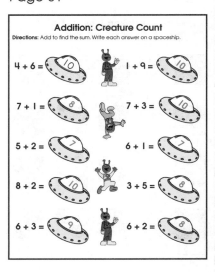

Addition: Creature Count

Directions: Add to find the sum. Write each answer on a spaceship.

4 + 6 = 10   1 + 9 = 10

7 + 1 = 8   7 + 3 = 10

5 + 2 = 7   6 + 1 = 7

8 + 2 = 10   3 + 5 = 8

6 + 3 = 9   6 + 2 = 8

Summer Link Super Edition Grade 2

Page 32

Addition: Lumberjack Facts

Directions: Add to find the sum. Use the code to color the picture.

Code:
1 — red   3 — black   5 — brown
2 — yellow   4 — blue   6 — green

What is it? __A beaver__

Page 33

Addition: Grid

Directions: Write the sums where the columns and rows meet. The first one shows you what to do.

+	1	2	3	4	5	6	7	8	9
1	2	3	4	5	6	7	8	9	10
2	3	4	5	6	7	8	9	10	11
3	4	5	6	7	8	9	10	11	12
4	5	6	7	8	9	10	11	12	13
5	6	7	8	9	10	11	12	13	14
6	7	8	9	10	11	12	13	14	15
7	8	9	10	11	12	13	14	15	16
8	9	10	11	12	13	14	15	16	17
9	10	11	12	13	14	15	16	17	18

Page 34

Addition: Math-Minded Mermaids

Directions: Look at each number. Then, look in each seashell. Circle each p of numbers that can be added together to equal that number.

Page 35

Addition: In the Doghouse

Directions: Look at the pictures. Complete the addition sentences.

Page 36

Addition: Practice

Directions: Add.

6 +4 = 10	7 +2 = 9	4 +4 = 8	4 +5 = 9	9 +1 = 10	3 +2 = 5
2 +7 = 9	6 +2 = 8	4 +0 = 4	2 +5 = 7	1 +4 = 5	4 +6 = 10
8 +1 = 9	2 +2 = 4	3 +6 = 9	1 +7 = 8	7 +3 = 10	1 +8 = 9
2 +3 = 5	2 +8 = 10	3 +5 = 8	8 +2 = 10	6 +1 = 7	0 +9 = 9
1 +9 = 10	6 +3 = 9	3 +4 = 7	5 +2 = 7	5 +4 = 9	4 +3 = 7
5 +3 = 8	8 +0 = 8	5 +5 = 10	3 +7 = 10	2 +6 = 8	3 +3 = 6

Page 37

Addition: Facts Through 12

Directions: Add.

2 +9 = 11	9 +2 = 11	3 +8 = 11	8 +3 = 11
5 +6 = 11	6 +5 = 11	4 +7 = 11	7 +4 = 11
8 +4 = 12	4 +8 = 12	7 +5 = 12	5 +7 = 12
9 +3 = 12	3 +9 = 12	6 +6 = 12	

Directions: Add.

8 +3 = 11	6 +6 = 12	9 +3 = 12	3 +8 = 11	4 +7 = 11	2 +9 = 11
5 +7 = 12	8 +4 = 12	7 +5 = 12	5 +6 = 11	9 +2 = 11	4 +8 = 12

Page 38

Subtraction: Secrets

Directions: Solve the subtraction problems. Use the code to find the secret message.

Code:

PLEASE, DON'T EVER

8 -3 = 5	10 -7 = 3	9 -2 = 7	10 -4 = 6	9 -6 = 3	6 -2 = 4	7 -4 = 3	8 -6 = 2
T	A	K	E	A	W	A	Y

MY MATH!

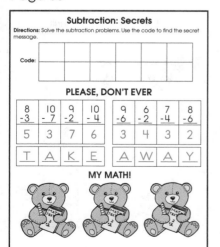

Page 39

Subtraction: Facts Through 12

Directions: Subtract.

11 -9 = 2	11 -2 = 9	11 -8 = 3	11 -3 = 8
11 -6 = 5	11 -5 = 6	11 -7 = 4	11 -4 = 7
12 -8 = 4	12 -4 = 8	12 -7 = 5	12 -5 = 7
12 -9 = 3	12 -3 = 9	12 -6 = 6	

Subtract.

11 -3 = 8	11 -6 = 5	12 -3 = 9	11 -8 = 3	12 -7 = 5	12 -9 = 3
11 -7 = 4	12 -4 = 8	12 -5 = 7	12 -6 = 6	11 -2 = 9	12 -8 = 4

Page 40

Subtraction: Practice

Directions: Subtract.

9 -4 = 5	7 -6 = 1	10 -5 = 5	9 -7 = 2	8 -5 = 3	10 -9 = 1
10 -4 = 6	6 -3 = 3	9 -6 = 3	10 -3 = 7	9 -0 = 9	5 -1 = 4
3 -1 = 2	9 -1 = 8	10 -8 = 2	7 -2 = 5	9 -5 = 4	2 -2 = 0
10 -1 = 9	7 -0 = 7	5 -3 = 2	8 -7 = 1	10 -2 = 8	6 -4 = 2
9 -8 = 1	7 -4 = 3	10 -0 = 10	4 -2 = 2	8 -4 = 4	9 -3 = 6
10 -6 = 4	8 -6 = 2	9 -2 = 7	8 -1 = 7	9 -9 = 0	10 -7 = 3

Page 41

Addition and Subtraction

Directions: Solve the number problem under each picture. Write + or – to show if you should add or subtract.

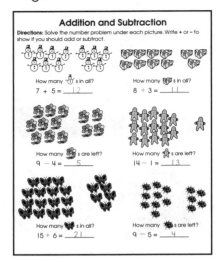

How many ☃ s in all?
7 + 5 = 12

How many 🍪 s in all?
8 + 3 = 11

How many 🍪 s are left?
9 – 4 = 5

How many 🍪 s are left?
14 – 1 = 13

How many 🦋 s in all?
15 + 6 = 21

How many 🐞 s are left?
9 – 5 = 4

Page 42

Addition and Subtraction

Directions: Add or subtract.
If you get 9, color the part red. If you get 14, color the part brown.

9 −7 = 2	3 +4 = 7	12 −8 = 4

5 + 5 = 10

| 15 −8 = 7 | 14 −9 = 5 |

11 – 7 = 4

14 – 5 = 9   7 – 6 = 1

8 +6 = 14   6 −5 = 1

18 −9 = 9   11 −3 = 8   6 +3 = 9

4 + 8 = 12

13 −4 = 9   2 +7 = 9   17 −8 = 9

4 +5 = 9   16 −7 = 9

12 −3 = 9

15 −6 = 9   13 −8 = 5

5 +9 = 14

7 +7 = 14   9 +5 = 14

6 +8 = 14

5 +6 = 11   10 −7 = 3   6 +6 = 12   8 +9 = 17   11 −5 = 6   9 +7 = 16   8 +8 = 16

Page 43

Addition and Subtraction

Directions:
Add.

5 +4 = 9	4 +3 = 7	1 +2 = 3	5 +3 = 8	4 +6 = 10	4 +4 = 8
0 +6 = 6	4 +1 = 5	8 +1 = 9	9 +1 = 10	8 +2 = 10	2 +2 = 4
2 +7 = 9	5 +2 = 7	1 +6 = 7	5 +5 = 10	4 +5 = 9	6 +2 = 8

Subtract.

10 −6 = 4	8 −2 = 6	5 −3 = 2	7 −6 = 1	4 −3 = 1	10 −5 = 5
9 −3 = 6	10 −2 = 8	7 −2 = 5	8 −6 = 2	10 −9 = 1	8 −8 = 0
10 −4 = 6	9 −6 = 3	9 −8 = 1	8 −1 = 7	10 −7 = 3	7 −4 = 3

Page 44

Addition: Review

Directions: Add.

24 +13 = 37	75 + 4 = 79	50 +27 = 77	62 +15 = 77	46 +23 = 69
52 +34 = 86	96 + 2 = 98	73 +16 = 89	38 +40 = 78	35 +21 = 56
10 +21 = 31	14 + 5 = 19	12 +34 = 46	33 +53 = 86	13 +11 = 24
24 +21 = 45	57 + 2 = 59	60 +33 = 93	12 +43 = 55	71 +26 = 97
16 +52 = 68	28 + 1 = 29	51 +27 = 78	40 +45 = 85	63 +16 = 79
22 +67 = 89	64 + 4 = 68	24 +72 = 96	41 +38 = 79	31 +56 = 87

Page 45

Subtraction: Review

Directions: Subtract.

75 −34 = 41	67 − 4 = 63	30 −20 = 10	48 −30 = 18	55 −32 = 23
78 −67 = 11	56 − 3 = 53	98 −86 = 12	86 −15 = 71	98 −48 = 50
95 −31 = 64	84 − 2 = 82	65 −45 = 20	79 −48 = 31	84 −50 = 34
42 −10 = 32	39 − 6 = 33	89 −42 = 47	67 −21 = 46	66 −36 = 30
98 −73 = 25	72 − 2 = 70	43 −13 = 30	57 −32 = 25	69 −15 = 54
32 −11 = 21	97 − 5 = 92	78 −22 = 56	99 −16 = 83	87 −47 = 40

Page 46

Place Value: Tens and Ones

The place value of a digit, or numeral, is shown by where it is in the number. For example, in the number **23**, **2** has the place value of **tens**, and **3** is **ones**.

Directions: Count the groups of ten crayons and write the number by the word **tens**. Count the other crayons and write the number by the word **ones**.

Example:

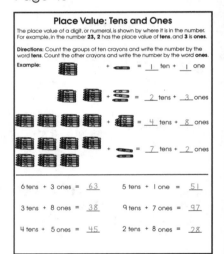

+ = 1 ten + 1 one

+ = 2 tens + 3 ones

+ = 4 tens + 8 ones

+ = 7 tens + 2 ones

6 tens + 3 ones = 63   5 tens + 1 one = 51

3 tens + 8 ones = 38   9 tens + 7 ones = 97

4 tens + 5 ones = 45   2 tens + 8 ones = 28

Page 47

Place Value: Ones, Tens

Directions: Write the numbers for the tens and ones. Then add.

Example:

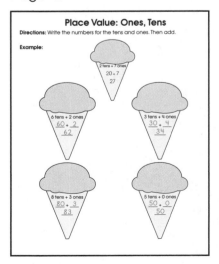

2 tens + 7 ones
20 + 7
27

6 tens + 2 ones
60 + 2
62

3 tens + 4 ones
30 + 4
34

8 tens + 3 ones
80 + 3
83

5 tens + 0 ones
50 + 0
50

Page 48

Place Value: Hundreds

Directions: Write the numbers for hundreds, tens, and ones. Then add.

Example:

1 hundred + 4 tens + 6 ones
100 + 40 + 6
146

7 hundreds + 3 tens + 5 ones
700 + 30 + 5
735

3 hundreds + 1 ten + 9 ones
300 + 10 + 9
319

5 hundreds + 8 tens + 0 ones
500 + 80 + 0
580

9 hundreds + 0 tens + 7 ones
900 + 0 + 7
907

Page 49

Fractions: Whole and Half

A fraction is a number that names part of a whole, such as $\frac{1}{2}$ or $\frac{3}{4}$.

Directions: Color half of each object.

Example:

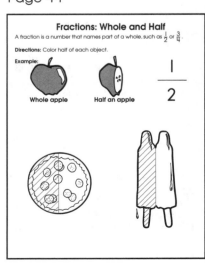

Whole apple   Half an apple $\frac{1}{2}$

Page 50

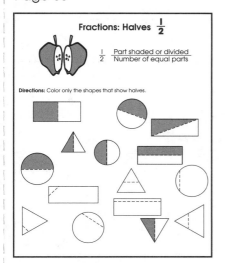

Page 51

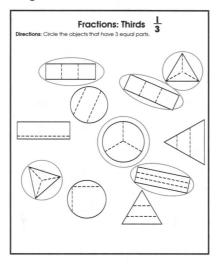

Page 52

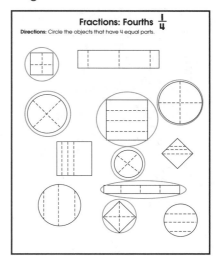

Page 53

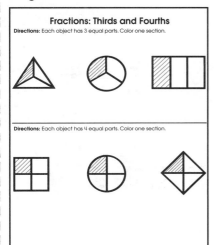

Page 54

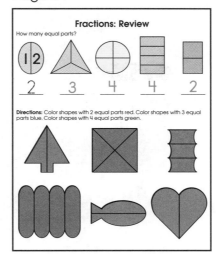

Page 55

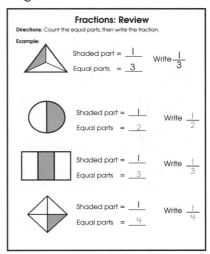

Page 56

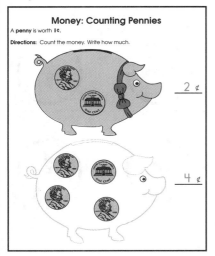

Page 57

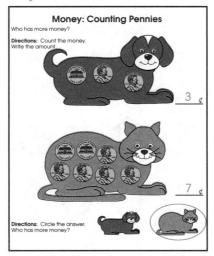

Page 58

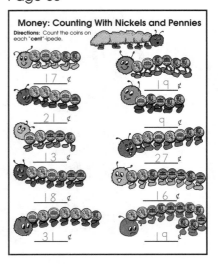

Summer Link Super Edition Grade 2

Page 59

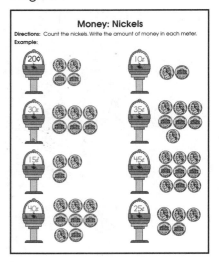

Page 60

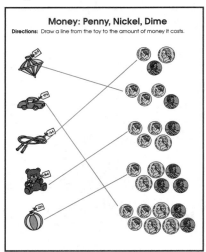

Page 61

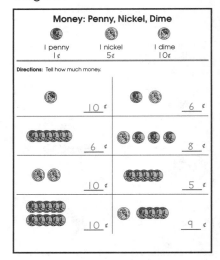

Page 62

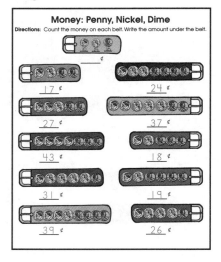

Page 63

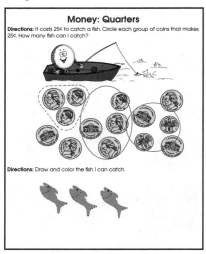

Page 64

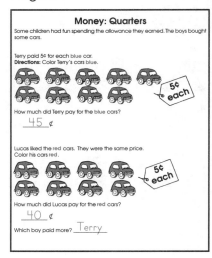

Page 65

Page 66

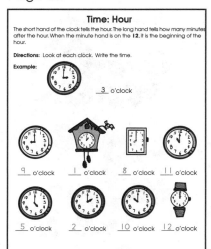

Page 67

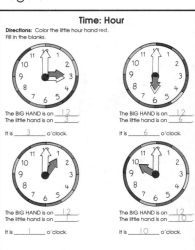

Page 68

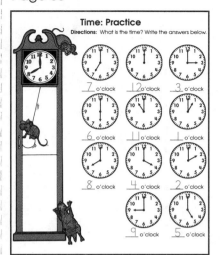

Time: Practice

Directions: What is the time? Write the answers below.

7 o'clock 12 o'clock 3 o'clock
6 o'clock 11 o'clock 1 o'clock
8 o'clock 4 o'clock 2 o'clock
9 o'clock 5 o'clock

Page 69

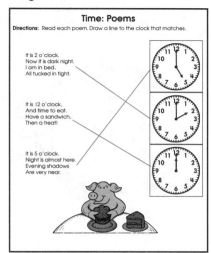

Time: Poems

Directions: Read each poem. Draw a line to the clock that matches.

It is 2 o'clock.
Now it is dark night.
I am in bed,
All tucked in tight.

It is 12 o'clock,
And time to eat.
Have a sandwich,
Then a treat!

It is 5 o'clock.
Night is almost here.
Evening shadows
Are very near.

Page 70

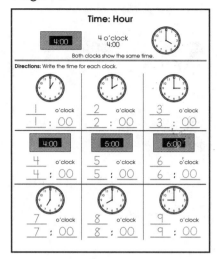

Time: Hour

4:00   4 o'clock
4:00

Both clocks show the same time.

Directions: Write the time for each clock.

1 o'clock 2 o'clock 3 o'clock
1 : 00   2 : 00   3 : 00

4:00   5:00   6:00
4 o'clock 5 o'clock 6 o'clock
4 : 00   5 : 00   6 : 00

7 o'clock 8 o'clock 9 o'clock
7 : 00   8 : 00   9 : 00

Page 71

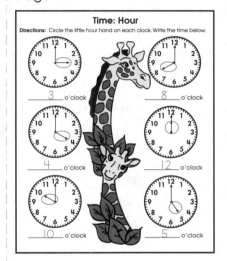

Time: Hour

Directions: Circle the little hour hand on each clock. Write the time below.

3 o'clock   8 o'clock
4 o'clock   12 o'clock
10 o'clock   5 o'clock

Page 72

Time: Hour, Half-Hour

An hour is sixty minutes. The short hand of a clock tells the hour. It is written 0:00, such as 5:00. A half-hour is thirty minutes. When the long hand of the clock is pointing to the 6, the time is on the half-hour. It is written :30, such as 5:30.

Directions: Study the examples. Tell what time it is on each clock.

Examples:

9:00
The minute hand is on the 12.
The hour hand is on the 9.
It is 9 o'clock.

4:30
The minute hand is on the 6.
The hour hand is between the 4 and 5. It is 4:30.

2:00   3:30   1:00   5:30   8:00
10:30 12:00 9:30   2:30   3:00

Page 73

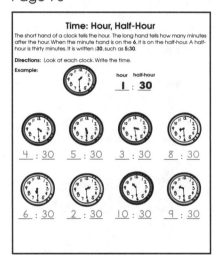

Time: Hour, Half-Hour

The short hand of a clock tells the hour. The long hand tells how many minutes after the hour. When the minute hand is on the 6, it is on the half-hour. A half-hour is thirty minutes. It is written :30, such as 5:30.

Directions: Look at each clock. Write the time.

Example:

hour half-hour
1 : 30

4 : 30   5 : 30   3 : 30   8 : 30
6 : 30   2 : 30   10 : 30 9 : 30

Page 74

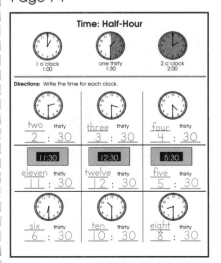

Time: Half-Hour

1 o'clock   one thirty   2 o'clock
1:00   1:30   2:00

Directions: Write the time for each clock.

two thirty   three thirty   four thirty
2 : 30   3 : 30   4 : 30

11:30   12:30   5:30
eleven thirty twelve thirty five thirty
11 : 30   12 : 30   5 : 30

six thirty   ten thirty   eight thirty
6 : 30   10 : 30   8 : 30

Page 75

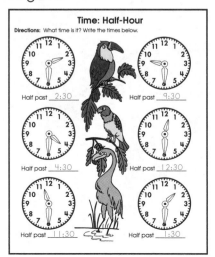

Time: Half-Hour

Directions: What time is it? Write the times below.

Half past 2:30   Half past 9:30
Half past 4:30   Half past 12:30
Half past 11:30   Half past 1:30

Page 76

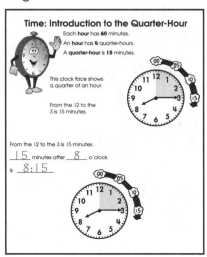

Time: Introduction to the Quarter-Hour

Each **hour** has **60** minutes.
An **hour** has **4** quarter-hours.
A **quarter-hour** is **15** minutes.

This clock face shows a quarter of an hour.

From the 12 to the 3 is 15 minutes.

From the 12 to the 3 is 15 minutes.

15 minutes after 8 o'clock
is 8:15

Page 77

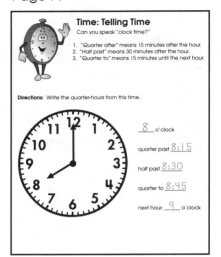

Time: Telling Time

Can you speak "clock time?"

1. "Quarter after" means 15 minutes after the hour.
2. "Half past" means 30 minutes after the hour.
3. "Quarter to" means 15 minutes until the next hour.

Directions: Write the quarter-hours from this time.

_8_ o'clock

quarter past _8:15_

half past _8:30_

quarter to _8:45_

next hour: _9_ o'clock

Page 78

Time: Counting by Fives

Directions: Fill in the numbers on the clock face. Count by fives around the clock.

There are ___ minutes in one hour.

Page 79

Time: Introduction to the Minute Intervals

Each number on the clock face stands for 5 minutes.

Directions: Count by 5's beginning at 12. Write the numbers here:

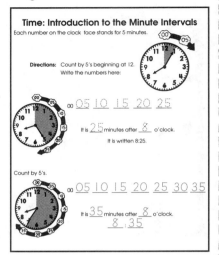

00 _05_ _10_ _15_ _20_ _25_

It is _25_ minutes after _8_ o'clock.

It is written 8:25.

Count by 5's.

00 _05_ _10_ _15_ _20_ _25_ _30_ _35_

It is _35_ minutes after _8_ o'clock.

_8_ : _35_

Page 80

Time: Introduction to the Minute Intervals

Directions: Write the time both ways.

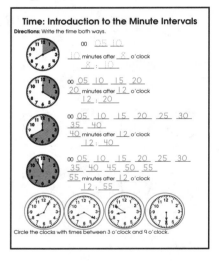

00 _05_ _10_

_10_ minutes after _8_ o'clock

_8_ : _10_

00 _05_ _10_ _15_ _20_

_20_ minutes after _12_ o'clock

_12_ : _20_

00 _05_ _10_ _15_ _20_ _25_ _30_ _35_ _40_

_40_ minutes after _12_ o'clock

_12_ : _40_

00 _05_ _10_ _15_ _20_ _25_ _30_ _35_ _40_ _45_ _50_ _55_

_55_ minutes after _12_ o'clock

_12_ : _55_

Circle the clocks with times between 3 o'clock and 9 o'clock.

Page 81

Time: Calendar

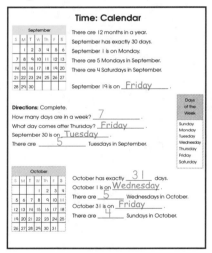

There are 12 months in a year.

September has exactly 30 days.

September 1 is on Monday.

There are 5 Mondays in September.

There are 4 Saturdays in September.

September 19 is on _Friday_.

Directions: Complete.

How many days are in a week? _7_.

What day comes after Thursday? _Friday_.

September 30 is on _Tuesday_.

There are _5_ Tuesdays in September.

Days of the Week

Sunday
Monday
Tuesday
Wednesday
Thursday
Friday
Saturday

October has exactly _31_ days.

October 1 is on _Wednesday_.

There are _5_ Wednesdays in October.

October 31 is on _Friday_.

There are _4_ Sundays in October.

Page 82

Time: Calendar

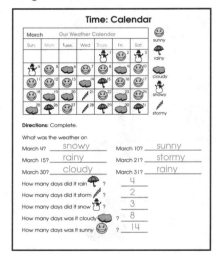

Directions: Complete.

What was the weather on

March 4? _snowy_   March 10? _sunny_

March 15? _rainy_   March 21? _stormy_

March 30? _cloudy_   March 31? _rainy_

How many days did it rain? _4_

How many days did it storm? _2_

How many days did it snow? _3_

How many days was it cloudy? _8_

How many days was it sunny? _14_

Page 83

Graphs

A graph is a drawing that shows information about numbers.

Directions: Count the apples in each row. Color the boxes to show how many apples have bites taken out of them.

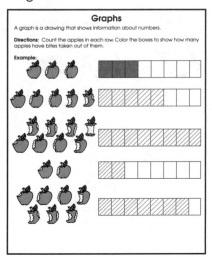

Example:

Page 84

Graphs

Directions: Count the fish. Color the bowls to make a graph that shows the number of fish.

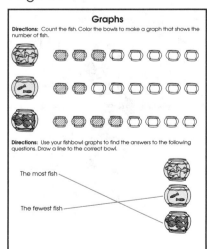

Directions: Use your fishbowl graphs to find the answers to the following questions. Draw a line to the correct bowl.

The most fish

The fewest fish

Page 85

Greater Than, Less Than

Directions: In each shape, circle the smallest number. Draw a square around the largest number.

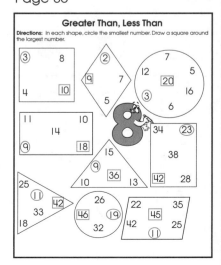

Page 86

Greater Than, Less Than

Directions: The open mouth points to the larger number. The small point goes to the smaller number. Draw the symbol < or > to the correct number.

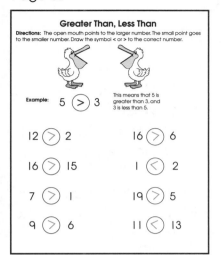

Example: 5 ⬭>⬭ 3   This means that 5 is greater than 3, and 3 is less than 5.

12 (>) 2   16 (>) 6

16 (>) 15   1 (<) 2

7 (>) 1   19 (>) 5

9 (>) 6   11 (<) 13

Page 87

Greater Than, Less Than

Directions: Write < or > in each circle. Make sure the "mouth" is open toward the greater number.

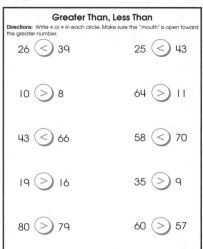

26 (<) 39   25 (<) 43

10 (>) 8   64 (>) 11

43 (<) 66   58 (<) 70

19 (>) 16   35 (>) 9

80 (>) 79   60 (>) 57

Page 88

Measurement: The Inch Worm

Directions: Use an inch ruler to measure these worms to the nearest inch.

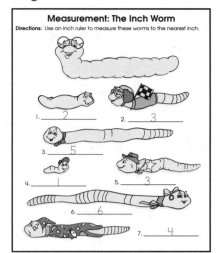

1. 2
2. 3
3. 5
4. 1
5. 3
6. 6
7. 4

Page 89

Measurement: Inches

An **inch** is a unit of length in the standard measurement system.

Directions: Use a ruler to measure each object to the nearest inch.

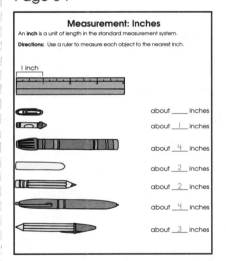

about ___ inches
about 1 inches
about 4 inches
about 2 inches
about 2 inches
about 4 inches
about 3 inches

Page 90

Measurement: Inches

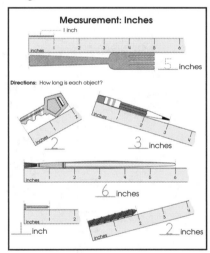

5 inches

Directions: How long is each object?

2   3 inches

6 inches

1 inch   2 inches

Page 91

Measurement: Measuring

Directions: Work with a friend. Use a centimeter ruler. Measure each other.

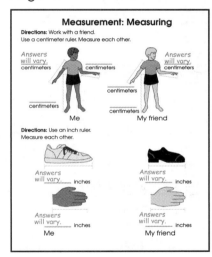

Answers will vary. centimeters   Answers will vary. centimeters

centimeters

centimeters   centimeters

Me   My friend

Directions: Use an inch ruler. Measure each other.

Answers will vary. inches   Answers will vary. inches

Answers will vary. inches   Answers will vary. inches

Me   My friend

Page 92

Measurement: Centimeters

A **centimeter** is a unit of length in the metric system. There are 2.54 centimeters in an inch.

Directions: Use a centimeter ruler to measure the crayons to the nearest centimeter.

Example: The first crayon is about 7 centimeters long.

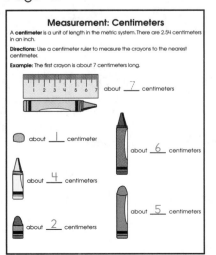

about 7 centimeters

about 1 centimeter

about 6 centimeters

about 4 centimeters

about 5 centimeters

about 2 centimeters

Page 93

Measurement: Centimeters

Directions: The giraffe is about 8 centimeters high. How many centimeters (cm) high are the trees? Write your answers in the blanks.

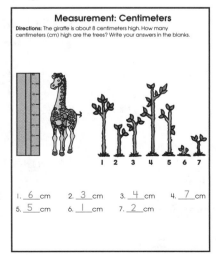

1. 6 cm   2. 3 cm   3. 4 cm   4. 7 cm
5. 5 cm   6. 1 cm   7. 2 cm

Page 94

Measurement: Centimeters

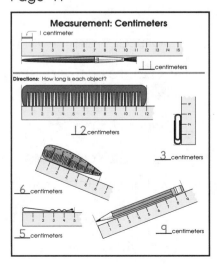

1 centimeter

11 centimeters

Directions: How long is each object?

12 centimeters

3 centimeters

6 centimeters

5 centimeters   9 centimeters

Developmental Skills for Second Grade Math Success

Parents and educators alike know that the School Specialty name ensures outstanding educational experience and content. Summer Link Math was designed to help your child retain those skills learned during the past school year. With Summer Link Math, your child will be ready to review and take on new material with confidence when he or she returns to school in the fall. The skills reviewed here will help your child be prepared for proficiency testing.

You can use this checklist to evaluate your child's progress. Place a check mark in the box if the appropriate skill has been mastered. If your child needs more work with a particular skill, place an "R" in the box and come back to it for review.

Math Skills

☐ Counts to 100

☐ Recognizes numbers up to 100

☐ Counts by 2s to 100

☐ Counts by 5s to 100

☐ Counts by 10s to 100

☐ Sorts objects using at least one attribute

☐ Can add up to 10

☐ Can write simple sentences using + and −

☐ Can subtract from 10

☐ Indicates order using ordinal numbers

☐ Can add up to 18

☐ Can subtract from 18

Understands and writes numbers

    ☐ with a place value in the ones

    ☐ with a place value in the tens

☐ Completes two-digit addition; no regrouping

☐ Completes two-digit subtraction; no regrouping

☐ Performs 3 single-digit column addition

☐ Recognizes coins

☐ Knows values of coins

☐ Can tell the value of coin combinations

☐ Can write simple money addition problems

☐ Knows 60 seconds are in a minute

☐ Knows 60 minutes make up an hour

☐ Uses less than and more than to interpret amounts

☐ Can name fractions of $\frac{1}{4}$, $\frac{1}{3}$, and $\frac{1}{2}$

☐ Uses problem-solving strategies

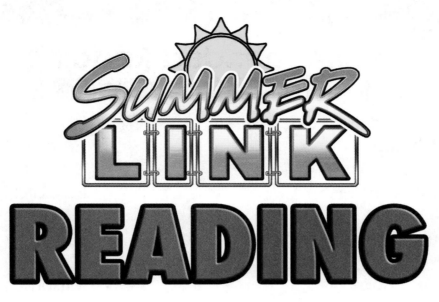

READING

Recommended Reading
Summer Before Grade 2

- **Amelia Bedelia Series**   Herman Parish

- **Animal Close-Ups Series**   Barbara Taylor

- **Animals Should Definitely Not Wear Clothing**   Judy Barrett

- **Anno's Counting Book**   Mitsumasa Anno

- **The Arctic; The Desert; The Ocean; The Rain Forest**   Alan Baker

- **Arthur Series**   Marc Brown

- **Berenstain Bears Series**   Stan and Jan Berenstain

- **Chester's Way; Julius, the Baby of the World**   Kevin Henkes

- **Chicken Man**   Michelle Edwards

- **Dandelions**   Eve Bunting

- **Elizabeth & Larry**   Marilyn Sadler

- **Emma**   Wendy Kesselman

- **Emmett's Dream;**
  Molly and Emmett's Camping Adventure;
  Molly and Emmett's Surprise Garden   Marylin Hafner

- **Fox In Love** (first readers)   Edward Marshall

- **George and Martha Series** (first readers)   James Marshall

- **Henry and Mudge Series** (first readers)   Cynthia Rylant

- **Ira Says Goodbye**   Bernard Waber

- **Little Critter Series** (first readers)   Mercer Mayer

- **My Friend Rabbit**   Eric Rohman

- **The Napping House**   Audrey and Don Wood

- **Noisy Nora**   Rosemary Wells

- **Tuesday**   David Wiesner

- **The Very Quiet Cricket**   Eric Carle

- **Who Sank the Boat ?**   Pamela Allen

- **Why Mosquitoes Buzz In People's Ears**   Verna Aardema

- **The World That Jack Built**   Ruth Brown

Name _____

Review the Alphabet

Directions: Practice writing the letters.

Aa

Bb

Cc

Dd

Review the Alphabet

Directions: Practice writing the letters.

Ee

Ff

Gg

Hh

Review the Alphabet

Directions: Practice writing the letters.

Name _____

Review the Alphabet

Directions: Practice writing the letters.

Mm

- -

- -

Nn

- -

- -

Oo

- -

- -

Pp

- -

- -

Review the Alphabet

Directions: Practice writing the letters.

Review the Alphabet

Directions: Practice writing the letters.

Review the Alphabet

Directions: Practice writing the letters.

Name _____

ABC Order

Directions: Circle the first letter of each word. Then put each pair of the words in abc order.

ⓒar   ⓑird   moon   two   nest   fan

bird

car

card   dog   pig   bike   sun   pie

Beginning Sounds

Directions: Say the sound of the letter at the beginning of each row. Find the pictures in each row that begin with the same letter. Write the letter under the pictures.

Example:

h

        _____   h   h   _____

f

        _____   _____   _____   _____

l

        _____   _____   _____   _____

n

        _____   _____   _____   _____

Beginning Sounds

Directions: Say the name of each thing. Write the beginning sound under its name. Find two pictures in each row that begin with the same sound as the first picture. Write the same first letter under them.

Example:

car
___C___   ___C___   _____   ___C___   _____

truck
_____   _____   _____   _____   _____

train
_____   _____   _____   _____   _____

bike
_____   _____   _____   _____   _____

  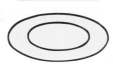

plane
_____   _____   _____   _____   _____

Summer Link Super Edition Grade 2

Name _____

Beginning Sounds

Directions: Use the sense words in the box to answer each question.

smell	see	taste	hear	touch

1. Which word begins with the same sound as

_____

2. Which word begins with the same sound as

_____

3. Which words begin with the same sound as

_____   _____

4. Which word begins with the same sound as

_____

Name _____

Beginning Sounds

Directions: Write the food names that answer the questions.

| egg | milk | ice cream | apple | cookie | cake |

1. Which food words start with the same sounds as the pictures?

-------------------------   --------------------------

----

2. Which food word ends with the same sound as the picture?

----

3. Which food words have two letters together that are the same?

------------------   ------------------   ------------------

Beginning Sounds

Directions: Say the name of each animal. Write the beginning sound under its name. Find two pictures in each row that begin with the same sound as the animal. Write the same first letter under them.

Example:

frog
f
_____

f
_____

_____

f
_____

_____

cat
_____

_____

_____

_____

_____

fish
_____

_____

_____

_____

_____

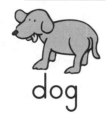
dog
_____

_____

_____

_____

_____

bird
_____

_____

_____

_____

_____

Beginning and Ending Sounds

Directions: Write the action words that answer the questions.

| sit | run | make | see | jump | stop | play | ride |

1. Which words begin with the same sound as ?

- -

2. Which words begin with the same sound as ?

- -

3. Which words begin with the same sound as each of these words?

- -

4. Which words end with the same sound as these?

- -

Rhyming Words

Short a is the sound you hear in the word **math**.

Directions: Use the **short a** words in the box to write rhyming words.

lamp	fat	bat	van
path	can	cat	Dan
math	stamp	fan	sat

1. Write four words that rhyme with **mat**.

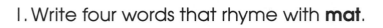

_____   _____

_____   _____

2. Write two words that rhyme with **bath**.

_____   _____

3. Write two words that rhyme with **damp**.

_____   _____

4. Write four words that rhyme with **pan**.

_____   _____

_____   _____

Spelling

Directions: Trace the letters to write the name of each food word. Write each name again by yourself. Then color the pictures.

Example:

bread **bread**

cookie

apple

cake

milk

egg

Name _____

Spelling

Directions: Write the correct number words in the blanks.

one	two	three	four	five	six	seven	eight	nine	ten

Add a letter to each of these words to make a number word.

Example:

even   on   tree

seven   _____   _____

Change a letter to make these words into number words.

Example:

live   fix   line

five   _____   _____

Write the number words that sound the same as these:

Example:

ate   to   for

_____   _____

Write the number word you did not use: _____

Spelling

Directions: The letters in the name of each thing are mixed up. Unscramble the letters and write each word correctly below.

Example:

   r a c   **car**

   a i t r n

   e p l n a

   k i b e

   c k u t r

Color the Eggs

Directions: Read the words. Color the picture with the correct colors.

Colorful Puzzle

Directions: Complete each color name. Some words go down and some go across.

y
b
e
l
b l
g o
b w
r

Summer Link Super Edition Grade 2

Capital Letters

Directions: A sentence begins with a capital letter. The words by each picture are mixed up. Write them to make a sentence that tells about the picture. Begin each sentence with a capital letter and end it with a period.

Example: coat she has a red

She has a red coat.

1. box sees he a blue

_____

- -

2. her is yellow flower

_____

- -

3. red draws he a door

_____

- -

Name _____

Days of the Week

Directions: The days of the week begin with capital letters. Write the days of the week in the spaces below. Put them in order. Be sure to start with capital letters.

Tuesday
Saturday
Monday
Friday
Thursday
Sunday
Wednesday

129   **Summer Link Super Edition Grade 2**

Name _____

Months of the Year

Directions: The months of the year begin with capital letters. Write the months of the year in order on the calendar below. Be sure to use capital letters.

January	December	April	May	October	June
September	February	July	March	November	August

_____

_____

_____

_____

_____

_____

_____

_____

_____

_____

_____

_____

Spelling Concentration Game

Directions: Play this game with a friend. Cut out each word card below and on pages 133 and 135. Lay the cards facedown on a flat surface. Take turns turning over two cards at a time. If the cards match, give the pair to your friend. Then spell the word from memory. If you spelled it correctly, you can keep the pair. If not, put the cards back facedown. When all of the word cards have been matched and spelled correctly, the players count their pairs. Whoever has the most pairs, wins.

You can also play this by yourself—or with more than one friend!

		dust
light	clean	bump
dust	sleep	clean
bump	light	sleep

This page is blank for cutting
exercise on previous page.

Spelling Concentration Game

note	head	write
soap	made	nine
stop	play	grew
clock	stamp	cute
tent	math	choose

This page is blank for cutting
exercise on previous page.

Spelling Concentration Game

note	head	write
soap	made	nine
stop	play	grew
clock	stamp	cute
tent	math	choose

This page is blank for cutting
exercise on previous page.

Plurals

Plurals are words that mean more than one. You usually add an **s** or **es** to the word. In some words ending in **y**, the **y** changes to an **i** before adding **es**. For example, **baby** changes to **babies**.

Directions: Look at the following lists of plural words. Write the word that means one next to it. The first one has been done for you.

foxes	**fox**	balls	_____
bushes	_____	candies	_____
dresses	_____	wishes	_____
chairs	_____	boxes	_____
shoes	_____	ladies	_____
stories	_____	bunnies	_____
puppies	_____	desks	_____
matches	_____	dishes	_____
cars	_____	pencils	_____
glasses	_____	trucks	_____

Name _____

Plurals

Directions: An **s** at the end of a word often means there is more than one. Look at each picture. Circle the correct word. Write the word on the line.

two
dog   dogs

- - - - - - - - - - - - - - - - - -

four
flower   flowers

- - - - - - - - - - - - - - - - - -

one
bikes   bike

- - - - - - - - - - - - - - - - - -

three
toys   toy

- - - - - - - - - - - - - - - - - -

a
lamb   lambs

- - - - - - - - - - - - - - - - - -

two
cat   cats

- - - - - - - - - - - - - - - - - -

Action Words

Directions: Action words tell things we can do. Trace the letters to write each action word. Then write the action word again by yourself.

Example:

sleep   sleep

run

make

ride

play

stop

Name _____

Action Words

Directions: Fill in the missing letters for each word.

Example:

paint   paint

c_tch   cat___

c_lor   col___

ea__ ___   ___ __t

gr___ ___ ___   ___ ___ ___ow

fl__   ___ ___ ___y

Action Words

Directions: Circle the word that is spelled correctly. Then write the correct spelling in the blank.

Example:

seep
(sleep)
slep

sleep

paly
pay
play

seee
cee
see

rum
run
runn

jump
jumb
junp

mack
maek
make

Action Words

Directions: Read each sentence and write the correct words in the blanks.

Example:

go
sleep

I will **go** to bed and **sleep** all night.

1.
see
jump

The girls _____ the frogs _____ .

2.
sit
run

After the boys _____ , they _____ and rest.

3.
stop
play

They _____ at the park so they can _____ .

4.
ride
make

They will _____ a car to _____ in.

Verbs

Directions: Look at the picture and read the words. Write an action word in each sentence below.

1. The two boys like to _____ together.

2. The children _____ the soccer ball.

3. Some children like to _____ on the swing.

4. The girl can _____ very fast.

5. The teacher _____ the bell.

Predicates

The **predicate** is the part of the sentence that tells about the action.

Directions: Circle the predicate in each sentence.

Example: The boys ran on the playground.

(Think: The boys did what?)

1. The woman painted a picture.

2. The puppy chases his ball.

3. The students went to school.

4. Butterflies fly in the air.

5. The baby wants a drink.

Compound Predicates

A **compound predicate** is made by joining two sentences that have the same subject. The predicates are joined together by the word **and**.

Example: Tom can jump.
              Tom can run.

Tom can <u>run</u> **and** <u>jump</u>.

Directions: Combine the sentences. Write the new sentence on the line.

1. The dog can roll over.
   The dog can bark.

_____

2. My mom plays with me.
   My mom reads with me.

_____

3. Tara is tall.
   Tara is smart.

_____

Nouns and Verbs

A **noun** is a person or thing a sentence tells about. A **verb** tells what the person or thing does.

Directions: Circle the noun in each sentence. Underline the verb.

Example: The (cat) sleeps.

1. Jill plays a game on the computer.

2. Children swim in the pool.

3. The car raced around the track.

4. Mike throws the ball to his friend.

5. Monkeys swing in the trees.

6. Terry laughed at the clown.

Name _____

Opposites

Opposites are things that are different in every way.

Directions: Draw a line between the opposites.

day

happy

big

open

front

little

closed

night

back

sad

Summer Link Super Edition Grade 2

Name _____

Antonyms

Antonyms are words that are opposites. **Hot** and **cold** are antonyms.

Directions: Draw lines to connect the words that are opposites.

up	wet
over	down
dry	dirty
clean	under

Antonyms

Directions: Find the two words that are opposites. Cut out the balloon basket and glue it on the proper balloon.

cut ✂ —

| slow | weak | dark | short |

This page is blank for cutting
exercise on previous page.

Antonyms

Directions: Draw a line between the antonyms.

closed

below

full

empty

above

old

new

open

Synonyms

Synonyms are words that have the same meaning.

Directions: Read each sentence and look at the underlined word. Circle the word that means the same thing. Write the new words.

1. The <u>little</u> dog ran.   tall   funny   small

2. The <u>happy</u> girl smiled.   glad   sad   good

3. The bird is in the <u>big</u> tree.   green   pretty   tall

4. He was <u>nice</u> to me.   kind   mad   bad

5. The baby is <u>tired</u>.   sleepy   sad   little

Name _____

Synonyms

Directions: Read the word in the center of each flower. Find a synonym for each word on a bee at the bottom of the page. Cut out and glue each bee on its matching flower.

cut ✂ -

This page is blank for cutting
exercise on previous page.

Similarities: Synonyms

Directions: Read each sentence. Read the word after the sentence. Find the word that is most like it in the sentence and circle it.

1. The flowers grew very tall.

 plants

2. Jan picked the apple from the tree.

 applesauce

3. Juan's van is dirty.

 truck

4. A dog makes a sound different from a cat.

 wolf

5. Dad put up a fence in the yard.

 gate

Synonyms

Directions: Read each sentence and look at the underlined word. Circle the word that means the same thing. Write the new words.

1. The boy was <u>mad</u>.	happy	angry	pup
2. The <u>dog</u> is brown.	pup	cat	rat
3. I like to <u>scream</u>.	soar	mad	shout
4. The bird can <u>fly</u>.	soar	jog	warm
5. The girl can <u>run</u>.	sleep	jog	shout
6. I am <u>hot</u>.	warm	cold	soar

1. _____   2. _____   3. _____

4. _____   5. _____   6. _____

Similarities: Synonyms

Directions: Read the story. Write a word on the line that means almost the same as the word under the line.

Dan went to the _____ .
store

He wanted to buy _____ .
food

He walked very _____ .
quickly

The store had what he wanted.

He bought it using _____ .
dimes

Instead of walking home, Dan _____ .
jogged

Synonyms

Directions: Circle the word in each row that is most like the first word in the row.

Example:

grin smile   frown   mad

bag jar   sack   box

cat fruit   animal   flower

apple rot   cookie   fruit

around  circle   square   dot

brown  tan   black   red

bird  dog   cat   duck

bee  fish   ant   snake

Name _____

Same and Different: These Don't Belong

Directions: Circle the pictures in each row that go together.

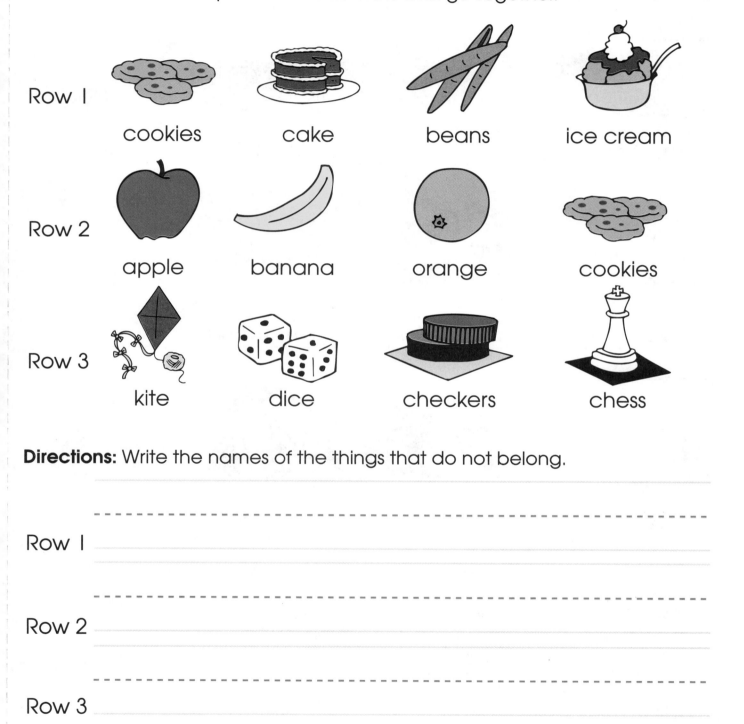

Row 1
cookies   cake   beans   ice cream

Row 2
apple   banana   orange   cookies

Row 3
kite   dice   checkers   chess

Directions: Write the names of the things that do not belong.

Row 1 _____

Row 2 _____

Row 3 _____

Summer Link Super Edition Grade 2

Similarities

Directions: Circle the picture in each row that is most like the first picture.

Example:

carrot   **jacks**   **bread**   **pea**

baseball   **sneakers**   **basketball**   **bat**

store   **school**   **home**   **bakery**

kitten   **dog**   **fox**   **cat**

Sentences and Non-Sentences

A **sentence** tells a complete idea. It has a noun and a verb. It begins with a capital letter and has punctuation at the end.

Directions: Circle the group of words if it is a sentence.

1. Grass is a green plant.

2. Mowing the lawn.

3. Grass grows in fields and lawns.

4. Tickle the feet.

5. Sheep, cows, and horses eat grass.

6. We like to play in.

7. My sister likes to mow the lawn.

8. A picnic on the grass.

9. My dog likes to roll in the grass.

10. Plant flowers around.

Sentences and Non-Sentences

Directions: Circle the group of words if it tells a complete idea.

1. A secret is something you know.

2. My mom's birthday gift is a secret.

3. No one else.

4. If you promise not to.

5. I'll tell you a secret.

6. Something nobody knows.

Statements

Statements are sentences that tell us something. They begin with a capital letter and end with a period.

Directions: Write the sentences on the lines below. Begin each sentence with a capital letter and end it with a period.

1. we like to ride our bikes

_____

2. we go down the hill very fast

_____

3. we keep our bikes shiny and clean

_____

4. we know how to change the tires

_____

Sentences

Directions: Read each sentence and write the correct words in the blanks.

Example:

taste
mouth

I can 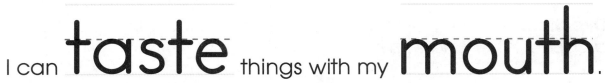 things with my **mouth**.

touch
hands

1. I can _____ things with my _____ .

nose
smell

2. I can _____ things with my _____ .

hear
ears

3. I can _____ with my _____ .

see
eyes

4. I can _____ things with my _____ .

Sentences

Directions: Write the food names in the story.

Kim got up in the morning.

"Do you want an _____ ⬤ ?" her mother asked.

"Yes, please," Kim said.

"May I have some _____ 🥛 , too?"

"Okay," her mother said.

"How about some _____ 🍦 ?" Kim asked with a smile.

Her mother laughed. "Not now," she said.

She put an _____ 🍎 in Kim's lunch.

"Do you want a _____ 🍪 or some

_____ 🍰 today?"

"Both!" Kim said.

Sentences

Directions: Read the sentence parts below. Draw a line from the first part of the sentence to the second part that completes it.

 1. I give big hugs

with my arms.

with my car.

 2. My feet

drive the car.

got wet in the rain.

 3. I have a bump

on my head.

on my coat.

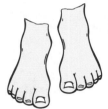 4. My mittens

keep my arms warm.

keep my hands warm.

 5. I can jump high

using my legs.

using a spoon.

Telling Sentences

Directions: Read the sentences and write them below. Begin each sentence with a capital letter. End each sentence with a period.

1. i like to go to the store with Mom
2. we go on Friday
3. i get to push the cart
4. i get to buy the cookies
5. i like to help Mom

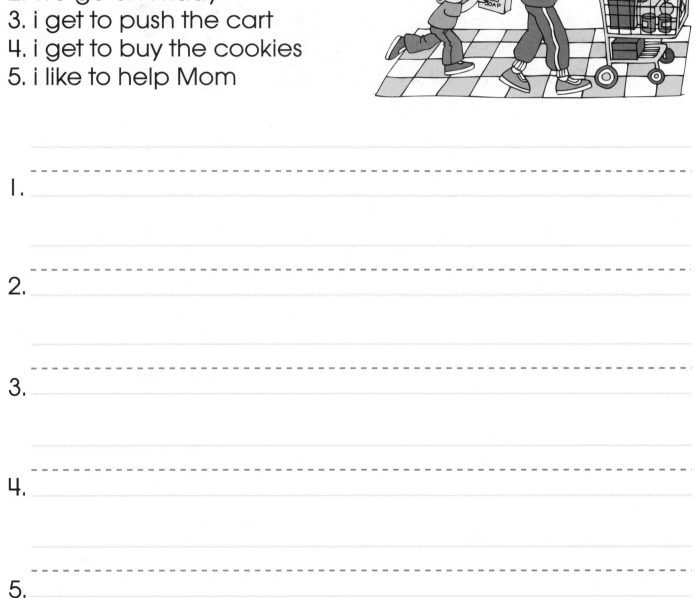

1. _____

2. _____

3. _____

4. _____

5. _____

Name _____

Telling Sentences

Directions: Read the sentences and write them below. Begin each sentence with a capital letter. End each sentence with a period.

1. most children like pets
2. some children like dogs
3. some children like cats
4. some children like snakes
5. some children like all animals

1. _____

2. _____

3. _____

4. _____

5. _____

Telling Sentences

Directions: Look at the pictures in each row. Write one sentence about the last picture in each row. Begin each sentence with a capital letter and end it with a period.

_____

- -

_____

_____

- -

_____

Asking Sentences

An **asking sentence** asks a question. Asking sentences end with a question mark.

Directions: Write each sentence on the line. Begin each sentence with a capital letter. Put a period at the end of the telling sentences and a question mark at the end of the asking sentences.

Example: do you like cake

Do you like cake?

1. the cow has spots

_____

2. is that cookie good

_____

3. she ate the apple

_____

Asking Sentences

Directions: Change each telling sentence into an asking sentence by moving the words. Put a question mark at the end of each question.

Example: The girl is eating.

 Is the girl eating?

 1. He is sharing.

_____

 2. He is drinking.

_____

 3. She is baking.

_____

Summer Link Super Edition Grade 2

Asking Sentences

Directions: Read the asking sentences. Write the sentences below. Begin each sentence with a capital letter. End each sentence with a question mark.

1. what game will we play
2. do you like to read
3. how old are you
4. who is your best friend
5. can you tie your shoes

1. _____

2. _____

3. _____

4. _____

5. _____

Name _____

Asking Sentences

Directions: Write the first word of each asking sentence. Be sure to begin each question with a capital letter. End each question with a question mark.

1. _____ you like the zoo   **do**

2. _____ much does it cost   **how**

3. _____ you feed the ducks   **can**

4. _____ you see the monkeys   **will**

5. _____ time will you eat lunch   **what**

Asking Sentences

Directions: Change each telling sentence into an asking sentence by moving the words. Put a question mark at the end of each question.

Example: He ate one cookie.

Is he eating one cookie?

1. She has two dogs.

---

2. Three balls can bounce.

---

3. One balloon is red.

Asking and Telling Sentences

Directions: Change the telling sentences into asking sentences. Change the asking sentences into telling sentences. Begin each one with a capital letter and end it with a period or a question mark.

Examples:

Is she eating three cookies?

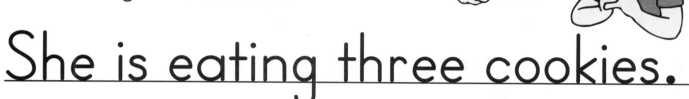

She is eating three cookies.

He is bringing one truck.

Is he bringing one truck?

1. Is he painting two blue birds?

_____

2. Did she find four apples?

_____

3. She will be six on her birthday.

_____

Name _____

Asking and Telling Sentences

Directions: Write the word that completes each sentence. Put a period at the end of the telling sentences and a question mark at the end of the asking sentences.

Example: I wear my hat on my **head.**

arms	legs	feet	hands

1. How strong are your _____ ☐

2. You wear shoes on your _____ ☐

3. If you're happy and you know it, clap your _____ ☐

4. My pants covered my _____ ☐

Asking and Telling Sentences

Directions: Write three telling sentences about the picture. Then write an asking sentence about the picture.

Telling sentences:

1. _____

2. _____

3. _____

Asking sentence:

_____

Asking and Telling Sentences

Directions: Write two telling sentences and one asking sentence about this picture. Use the food, color, and animal words you know.

Two telling sentences:

1. _____

2. _____

One asking sentence:

_____

Asking and Telling Sentences

Directions: Write two telling sentences and one asking sentence about this picture. Use the number words you know.

Two telling sentences:

1.

2.

One asking sentence:

Name _____

Following Directions

Directions: Look at the pictures. Follow the directions in each box.

Draw a circle around the caterpillar.
Draw a line under the stick.

Draw an **X** on the mother bird.
Draw a triangle around the baby birds.

Draw a box around the rabbit.

Color the flowers. Count the bees.
There are _____ bees.

Name _____

Following Directions: Play Simon Says

Directions: Read how to play Simon Says. Then answer the questions.

Simon Says

Here is how to play Simon Says:
One kid is Simon. Simon is the leader.
Everyone must do what Simon says
and does but only if the leader says,
"Simon says" first. Let'try it. "Simon
says, `Pat your head.'" "Simon says,
`Pat your nose. Pat your toes.'"
Oops! Did you pat your toes? I did not say, "Simon says," first.
If you patted your toes, you are out!

1. Who is the leader in this game?

2. What must the leader say first each time?

3. What happens if you do something and the leader did not say, "Simon says?"

Name _____

Following Directions: Play Simon Says

Directions: Read the sentences. If Simon tells you to do something, follow the directions. If Simon does not tell you to do something, go to the next sentence.

1. Simon says: Cross out all the numbers 2 through 9.

2. Simon says: Cross out the vowel that is in the word "sun."

3. Cross out the letter "B."

4. Cross out the vowels "A" and "E."

5. Simon says: Cross out the consonants in the word "cup."

6. Cross out the letter "Z."

7. Simon says: Cross out all the "K's."

8. Simon says: Read your message.

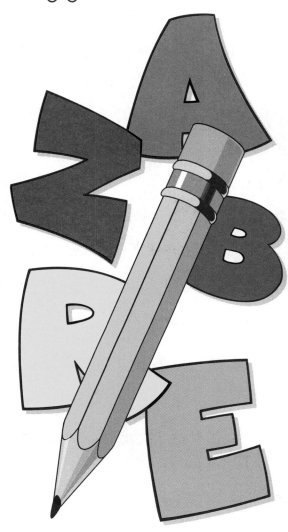

C 3 G U 7 P R U C P E K C P A 8 K K

6 T P U P J C 5 P O K 9 P B U P K K

Following Directions: Play Simon Says

Directions: Read each sentence. Look at the picture next to it. Circle the picture if the person is playing Simon Says correctly.

1. Simon says, "Put your hands on your hips."

2. Simon says, "Stand on one leg."

3. Simon says, "Put your hands on your head."

4. Simon says, "Ride a bike."

5. Simon says, "Jump up and down."

6. Simon says, "Pet a dog."

7. Simon says, "Make a big smile."

Name _____

Following Directions

Directions: Draw a hat on each person. Read the sentences to know what kind of hat to draw.

1. The second girl is wearing a purple hat with feathers.

2. The boy next to the girl with the purple hat is wearing a red baseball hat.

3. The first boy is wearing a yellow knit hat.

4. The last boy is wearing a brown top hat.

5. The girl next to the boy with the red hat is wearing a blue straw hat.

Following Directions

Directions: Color the path the girl should take to go home. Use the sentences to help you.

1. Go to the school and turn left.

2. At the end of the street, turn right.

3. Walk past the park and turn right.

4. After you pass the pool, turn right.

Name _____

Following Directions

Directions: Follow directions to complete the picture of the tiger.

1. Draw black stripes on the tiger's body and tail.

2. Color the tiger's tongue red.

3. Draw claws on the feet.

4. Draw a black nose and two black eyes on the tiger's face.

5. Color the rest of the tiger orange.

6. Draw tall, green grass for the tiger to sleep in.

Sequencing: Make an Ice-Cream Cone

Directions: Number the boxes in order to show how to make an ice-cream cone.

Sequencing: Eating a Cone

What if a person never ate an ice-cream cone? Could you tell them how to eat it? Think about what you do when you eat an ice-cream cone.

Directions: Write directions to teach someone how to eat an ice-cream cone.

How to Eat an Ice-Cream Cone

1. _____

2. _____

3. _____

4. _____

Sequencing: Choosing a Hat

Directions: Write a number in each box to show the order of the story.

Name _____

Classifying

Directions: Draw a ☐ around objects that are food for the party. Draw a △ around the party guests. Draw a ◯ around the objects used for fun at the party.

ice cream

candy

games

tiger

noise makers

cake

garbage can

cat

hat

glasses

candle

bear

juice

balloons

giraffe

pig

potato chips

hippo

Name _____

Classifying: What Does Not Belong?

Directions: Draw an **X** on the picture that does not belong in each group.

fruit

apple   peach   corn   watermelon

wild animals

bear   kitten   gorilla   lion

pets

cat   fish   elephant   dog

flowers

grass   rose   daisy   tulip

Name _____

Classifying

Directions: Color the meats and eggs brown. Color the fruits and vegetables green. Color the breads tan. Color the dairy foods (milk and cheese) yellow.

fish   bread   apple   cheese

crackers   carrot   orange   eggs

steaks   pear   milk   yogurt

ice cream   chicken   potato   pretzel

Classifying: A Rainy Day

Directions: Read the story. Then circle the objects Jonathan needs to stay dry.

It is raining. Jonathan wants to play outdoors. What should he wear to stay dry? What should he carry to stay dry?

Glossary of Reading and Language Arts Terms

adjective: a describing word that tells more about a noun

antonym: words with opposite, or nearly opposite, meanings

autobiography: a written account of your life

character: a person, animal, or object that a story is about

conclusion: a final decision about something, or the part of a story that tells what happens to the characters

fact: something known to be true

fiction: stories that are made up

nonfiction: stories that are true

noun: a word that names a person, place, or thing

opinion: a belief based on what a person thinks instead of what is known to be true

plot: explains the events in a story that create a problem

plural: a form of a word that names or refers to more than one person or thing

punctuation: the marks that qualify sentences, such as a period, comma, question mark, exclamation point, and apostrophe

reading strategies: a main idea, supporting details, context clues, fact/opinion

resolution: tells how the characters solve the story problem

setting: the place and time that a story happens

synonym: words that mean the same, or almost the same, thing

verb: a word that can show action

Page 115

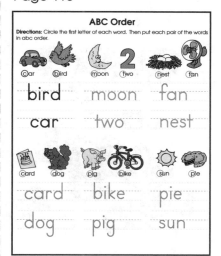

ABC Order

Directions: Circle the first letter of each word. Then put each pair of the words in abc order.

ⓒar ⓑird ⓜoon ⓣwo ⓝest ⓕan

bird   moon   fan
car   two   nest

ⓒard ⓓog ⓟig ⓑike ⓢun ⓟie

card   bike   pie
dog   pig   sun

Page 116

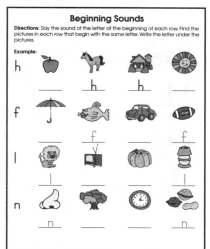

Beginning Sounds

Directions: Say the sound of the letter at the beginning of each row. Find the pictures in each row that begin with the same letter. Write the letter under the pictures.

Example:

h   h   h

f   f   f

l

n   n   n

Page 117

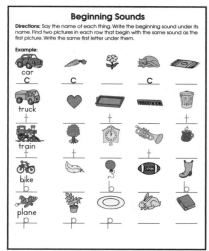

Beginning Sounds

Directions: Say the name of each thing. Write the beginning sound under its name. Find two pictures in each row that begin with the same sound as the first picture. Write the same first letter under them.

Example:

car   c   c   c
c

truck   t   t   t
t

train   t   t   t
t

bike   b   b   b
b

plane   p   p   p
p

Page 118

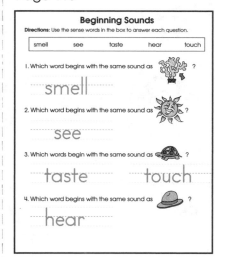

Beginning Sounds

Directions: Use the sense words in the box to answer each question.

| smell | see | taste | hear | touch |

1. Which word begins with the same sound as [image] ?

smell

2. Which word begins with the same sound as [image] ?

see

3. Which words begin with the same sound as [image] ?

taste   touch

4. Which word begins with the same sound as [image] ?

hear

Page 119

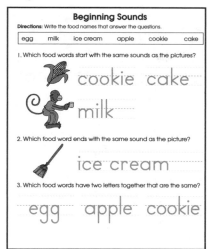

Beginning Sounds

Directions: Write the food names that answer the questions.

| egg | milk | ice cream | apple | cookie | cake |

1. Which food words start with the same sounds as the pictures?

cookie cake

milk

2. Which food word ends with the same sound as the picture?

ice cream

3. Which food words have two letters together that are the same?

egg   apple   cookie

Page 120

Beginning Sounds

Directions: Say the name of each animal. Write the beginning sound under its name. Find two pictures in each row that begin with the same sound as the animal. Write the same first letter under them.

Example:

frog   f   f   f
f

cat   c   c   c
c

fish   f   f   f
f

dog   d   d   d
d

bird   b   b   b
b

Page 121

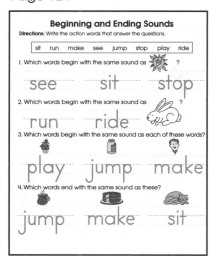

Beginning and Ending Sounds

Directions: Write the action words that answer the questions.

| sit | run | make | see | jump | stop | play | ride |

1. Which words begin with the same sound as [image] ?

see   sit   stop

2. Which words begin with the same sound as [image] ?

run   ride

3. Which words begin with the same sound as each of these words?

play   jump   make

4. Which words end with the same sound as these?

jump   make   sit

Page 122

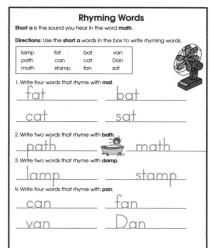

Rhyming Words

Short a is the sound you hear in the word **math**.

Directions: Use the **short a** words in the box to write rhyming words.

lamp	fat	bat	van
path	can	cat	Dan
math	stamp	fan	sat

1. Write four words that rhyme with **mat**.

fat   bat
cat   sat

2. Write two words that rhyme with **bath**.

path   math

3. Write two words that rhyme with **damp**.

lamp   stamp

4. Write four words that rhyme with **pan**.

can   fan
van   Dan

Page 123

Spelling

Directions: Trace the letters to write the name of each food word. Write each name again by yourself. Then color the pictures.

Example:

bread bread

cookie cookie

apple apple

cake cake

milk milk

egg egg

Page 124

Spelling

Directions: Write the correct number words in the blanks.

one two three four five six seven eight nine ten

Add a letter to each of these words to make a number word.

Example:

even	on	tree
seven	one	three

Change a letter to make these words into number words.

Example:

live	fix	line
five	six	nine

Write the number words that sound the same as these:

Example:

ate	to	for
eight	two	four

Write the number word you did not use: ten

Page 125

Spelling

Directions: The letters in the name of each thing are mixed up. Unscramble the letters and write each word correctly below.

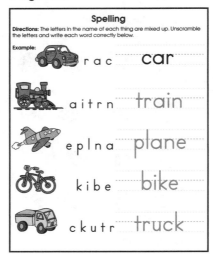

Example:

r a c — car

a i t r n — train

e p l n a — plane

k i b e — bike

c k u t r — truck

Page 126

Color the Eggs

Directions: Read the words. Color the picture with the correct colors.

Page 127

Colorful Puzzle

Directions: Complete each color name. Some words go down and some go across.

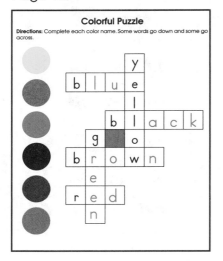

```
        y
  b l u e
      l
    b l a c k
    g   o
  b r o w n
    e
  r e d
    n
```

Page 128

Capital Letters

Directions: A sentence begins with a capital letter. The words by each picture tell about the picture. Write them to make a sentence that tells about the picture. Begin each sentence with a capital letter and end it with a period.

Example: coat she has a red

She has a red coat.

1. box sees he a blue

He sees a blue box.

2. her is yellow flower

Her flower is yellow.

3. red draws he a door

He draws a red door.

Page 129

Days of the Week

Directions: The days of the week begin with capital letters. Write the days of the week in the spaces below. Put them in order. Be sure to start with capital letters.

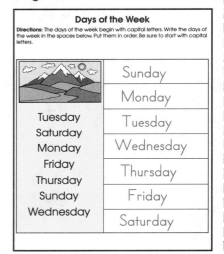

Tuesday	Sunday
Saturday	Monday
Monday	Tuesday
Friday	Wednesday
Thursday	Thursday
Sunday	Friday
Wednesday	Saturday

Page 130

Months of the Year

Directions: The months of the year begin with capital letters. Write the months of the year in order on the calendar below. Be sure to use capital letters.

January	December	April	May	October	June
September	February	July	March	November	August

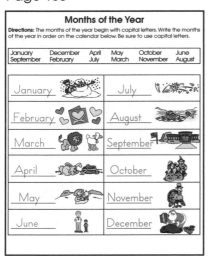

January	July
February	August
March	September
April	October
May	November
June	December

Page 137

Plurals

Plurals are words that mean more than one. You usually add an **s** or **es** to the word. In some words ending in **y**, the **y** changes to an **i** before adding **es**. For example, **baby** changes to **babies**.

Directions: Look at the following lists of plural words. Write the word that means one next to it. The first one has been done for you.

foxes	fox	balls	ball
bushes	bush	candies	candy
dresses	dress	wishes	wish
chairs	chair	boxes	box
shoes	shoe	ladies	lady
stories	story	bunnies	bunny
puppies	puppy	desks	desk
matches	match	dishes	dish
cars	car	pencils	pencil
glasses	glass	trucks	truck

Page 138

Plurals

Directions: An **s** at the end of a word often means there is more than one. Look at each picture. Circle the correct word. Write the word on the line.

two dog (dogs)	four flower (flowers)	one bikes (bike)
dogs	flowers	bike
three (toys) toy	a lamb (lamb) lambs	two cat (cats)
toys	lamb	cats

Page 139

Action Words

Directions: Action words tell things we can do. Trace the letters to write each action word. Then write the action word again by yourself.

Example:

sleep   sleep
run   run
make   make
ride   ride
play   play
stop   stop

Page 140

Action Words

Directions: Fill in the missing letters for each word.

Example:

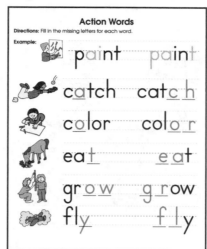

paint   paint
catch   catch
color   color
eat   eat
grow   grow
fly   fly

Page 141

Action Words

Directions: Circle the word that is spelled correctly. Then write the correct spelling in the blank.

Example:

seep / (sleep) / slep → sleep
paly / pay / (play) → play
seee / cee / (see) → see
rum / (run) / runn → run
(jump) / jumb / junp → jump
mack / maek / (make) → make

Page 142

Action Words

Directions: Read each sentence and write the correct words in the blanks.

Example:
go sleep → I will **go** to bed and **sleep** all night.

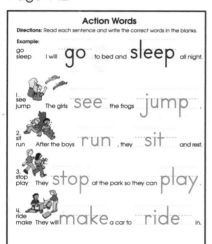

1. see jump → The girls **see** the frogs **jump**.
2. sit run → After the boys **run**, they **sit** and rest.
3. stop play → They **stop** at the park so they can **play**.
4. ride make → They will **make** a car to **ride** in.

Page 143

Verbs

Directions: Look at the picture and read the words. Write an action word in each sentence below.

1. The two boys like to **talk** together.
2. The children **kick** the soccer ball.
3. Some children like to **swing** on the swing.
4. The girl can **run** very fast.
5. The teacher **rings** the bell.

Page 144

Predicates

The **predicate** is the part of the sentence that tells about the action.

Directions: Circle the predicate in each sentence.

Example: The boys ran on the playground.
(Think: The boys did what? (Ran))

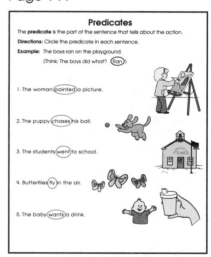

1. The woman (painted) a picture.
2. The puppy (chases) his ball.
3. The students (went) to school.
4. Butterflies (fly) in the air.
5. The baby (wants) a drink.

Page 145

Compound Predicates

A **compound predicate** is made by joining two sentences that have the same subject. The predicates are joined together by the word **and**.

Example: Tom can jump.
Tom can run.
Tom can run **and** jump.

Directions: Combine the sentences. Write the new sentence on the line.

1. The dog can roll over.
The dog can bark.
The dog can roll over and bark.

2. My mom plays with me.
My mom reads with me.
My mom plays and reads with me.

3. Tara is tall.
Tara is smart.
Tara is tall and smart.

Page 146

Nouns and Verbs

A **noun** is a person or thing a sentence tells about. A **verb** tells what the person or thing does.

Directions: Circle the noun in each sentence. Underline the verb.

Example: The (cat) sleeps.

1. (Jill) plays a game on the computer.
2. (Children) swim in the pool.
3. The (car) raced around the track.
4. (Mike) throws the ball to his friend.
5. (Monkeys) swing in the trees.
6. (Terry) laughed at the clown.

Page 147

Opposites

Opposites are things that are different in every way.

Directions: Draw a line between the opposites.

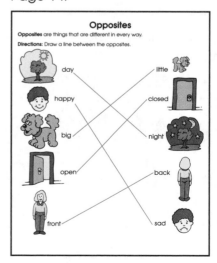

day — night
happy — sad
big — little
open — closed
front — back

197   Summer Link Super Edition Grade 2

Page 148

Antonyms

Antonyms are words that are opposites. **Hot** and **cold** are antonyms.

Directions: Draw lines to connect the words that are opposites.

up — wet
over — down
dry — dirty
clean — under

Page 149

Antonyms

Directions: Find the two words that are opposites. Cut out the balloon basket and glue it on the proper balloon.

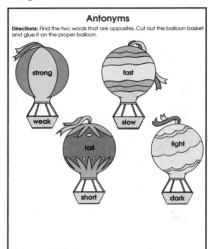

strong — weak
fast — slow
tall — short
light — dark

Page 151

Antonyms

Directions: Draw a line between the antonyms.

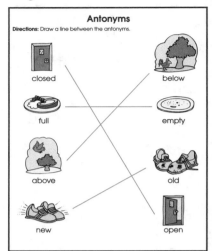

closed — open
full — empty
above — below
new — old

Page 152

Synonyms

Synonyms are words that have the same meaning.

Directions: Read each sentence and look at the underlined word. Circle the word that means the same thing. Write the new words.

1. The <u>little</u> dog ran.   tall   funny   (small)
2. The <u>happy</u> girl smiled.   (glad)   sad   good
3. The bird is in the <u>big</u> tree.   green   pretty   (tall)
4. He was <u>nice</u> to me.   (kind)   mad   bad
5. The baby is <u>tired</u>.   (sleepy)   sad   little

small   glad   tall
kind   sleepy

Page 153

Synonyms

Directions: Read the word in the center of each flower. Find a synonym for each word on a bee at the bottom of the page. Cut out and glue each bee on its matching flower.

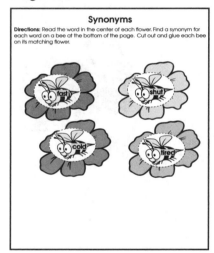

fast
shut
cold
tired

Page 155

Similarities: Synonyms

Directions: Read each sentence. Read the word after the sentence. Find the word that is most like it in the sentence and circle it.

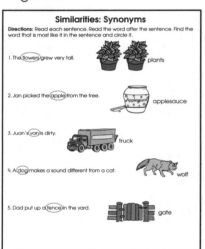

1. The (flowers) grew very tall.   plants
2. Jan picked the (apple) from the tree.   applesauce
3. Juan's (van) is dirty.   truck
4. A (dog) makes a sound different from a cat.   wolf
5. Dad put up a (fence) in the yard.   gate

Page 156

Synonyms

Directions: Read each sentence and look at the underlined word. Circle the word that means the same thing. Write the new words.

1. The boy was <u>mad</u>.   happy   (angry)   pup
2. The <u>dog</u> is brown.   (pup)   cat   rat
3. I like to <u>scream</u>.   soar   mad   (shout)
4. The bird can <u>fly</u>.   (soar)   jog   warm
5. The girl can <u>run</u>.   sleep   (jog)   shout
6. I am <u>hot</u>.   (warm)   cold   soar

1. angry   2. pup   3. shout
4. soar   5. jog   6. warm

Page 157

Similarities: Synonyms

Directions: Read the story. Write a word on the line that means almost the same as the word under the line.

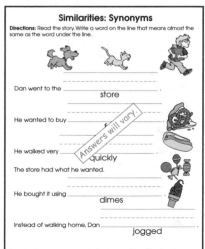

Dan went to the _____
   store

He wanted to buy _____

He walked very _____
   quickly

The store had what he wanted.

He bought it using _____
   dimes

Instead of walking home, Dan _____
   jogged

Answers will vary.

Page 158

Synonyms

Directions: Circle the word in each row that is most like the first word in the row.

Example:

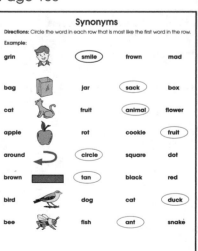

grin   (smile)   frown   mad
bag   jar   (sack)   box
cat   fruit   (animal)   flower
apple   rot   cookie   (fruit)
around   (circle)   square   dot
brown   (tan)   black   red
bird   dog   cat   (duck)
bee   fish   (ant)   snake

Page 159

Same and Different: These Don't Belong

Directions: Circle the pictures in each row that go together.

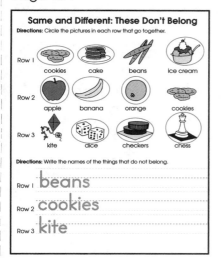

Row 1: cookies, cake, beans, ice cream
Row 2: apple, banana, orange, cookies
Row 3: kite, dice, checkers, chess

Directions: Write the names of the things that do not belong.

Row 1 beans
Row 2 cookies
Row 3 kite

Page 160

Similarities

Directions: Circle the picture in each row that is most like the first picture.

Example:

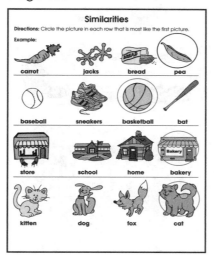

carrot, jacks, bread, pea
baseball, sneakers, basketball, bat
store, school, home, bakery
kitten, dog, fox, cat

Page 161

Sentences and Non-Sentences

A **sentence** tells a complete idea. It has a noun and a verb. It begins with a capital letter and has punctuation at the end.

Directions: Circle the group of words if it is a sentence.

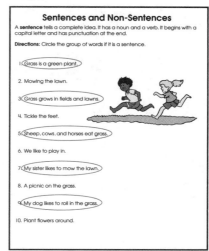

1. Grass is a green plant.
2. Mowing the lawn.
3. Grass grows in fields and lawns.
4. Tickle the feet.
5. Sheep, cows, and horses eat grass.
6. We like to play in.
7. My sister likes to mow the lawn.
8. A picnic on the grass.
9. My dog likes to roll in the grass.
10. Plant flowers around.

Page 162

Sentences and Non-Sentences

Directions: Circle the group of words if it tells a complete idea.

1. A secret is something you know.
2. My mom's birthday gift is a secret.
3. No one else.
4. If you promise not to.
5. I'll tell you a secret.
6. Something nobody knows.

Page 163

Statements

Statements are sentences that tell us something. They begin with a capital letter and end with a period.

Directions: Write the sentences on the lines below. Begin each sentence with a capital letter and end it with a period.

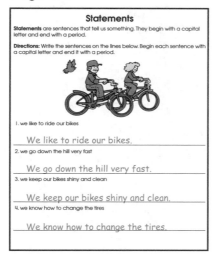

1. we like to ride our bikes
   We like to ride our bikes.
2. we go down the hill very fast
   We go down the hill very fast.
3. we keep our bikes shiny and clean
   We keep our bikes shiny and clean.
4. we know how to change the tires
   We know how to change the tires.

Page 164

Sentences

Directions: Read each sentence and write the correct words in the blanks.

Example:

taste / mouth — I can **taste** things with my **mouth**.

touch / hands — 1. I can **touch** things with my **hand**.
nose / smell — 2. I can **smell** things with my **nose**.
hear / ears — 3. I can **hear** with my **ear**.
see / eyes — 4. I can **see** things with my **eyes**.

Page 165

Sentences

Directions: Write the food names in the story.

Kim got up in the morning.

"Do you want an __egg__ ?" her mother asked.

"Yes, please," Kim said.

"May I have some __milk__ , too?"

"Okay," her mother said.

"How about some __ice cream__ ?" Kim asked with a smile.

Her mother laughed. "Not now," she said.

She put an __apple__ in Kim's lunch.

"Do you want a __cookie__ or some __cake__ today?"

"Both!" Kim said.

Page 166

Sentences

Directions: Read the sentence parts below. Draw a line from the first part of the sentence to the second part that completes it.

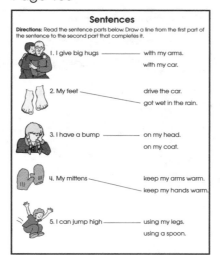

1. I give big hugs — with my arms.
   with my car.
2. My feet — drive the car.
   got wet in the rain.
3. I have a bump — on my head.
   on my coat.
4. My mittens — keep my arms warm.
   keep my hands warm.
5. I can jump high — using my legs.
   using a spoon.

Page 167

Telling Sentences

Directions: Read the sentences and write them below. Begin each sentence with a capital letter. End each sentence with a period.

1. i like to go to the store with Mom
2. we go on Friday
3. i get to push the cart
4. i get to buy the cookies
5. i like to help Mom

1. I like to go to the store with Mom.
2. We go on Friday.
3. I get to push the cart.
4. I get to buy the cookies.
5. I like to help Mom.

Page 168

Telling Sentences

Directions: Read the sentences and write them below. Begin each sentence with a capital letter. End each sentence with a period.

1. most children like pets
2. some children like dogs
3. some children like cats
4. some children like snakes
5. some children like all animals

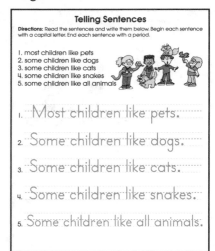

1. Most children like pets.
2. Some children like dogs.
3. Some children like cats.
4. Some children like snakes.
5. Some children like all animals.

Page 169

Telling Sentences

Directions: Look at the pictures in each row. Write one sentence about the last picture in each row. Begin each sentence with a capital letter and end it with a period.

Answers may include:

The cake is gone.

The barn is red.

Page 170

Asking Sentences

An **asking sentence** asks a question. Asking sentences end with a question mark.

Directions: Write each sentence on the line. Begin each sentence with a capital letter. Put a period at the end of the telling sentences and a question mark at the end of the asking sentences.

Example: do you like cake

Do you like cake?

1. the cow has spots

The cow has spots.

2. is that cookie good

Is that cookie good?

3. she ate the apple

She ate the apple.

Page 171

Asking Sentences

Directions: Change each telling sentence into an asking sentence by moving the words. Put a question mark at the end of each question.

Example: The girl is eating.

Is the girl eating?

1. He is sharing.

Is he sharing?

2. He is drinking.

Is he drinking?

3. She is baking.

Is she baking?

Page 172

Asking Sentences

Directions: Read the asking sentences. Write the sentences below. Begin each sentence with a capital letter. End each sentence with a question mark.

1. what game will we play
2. do you like to read
3. how old are you
4. who is your best friend
5. can you tie your shoes

1. What game will we play?
2. Do you like to read?
3. How old are you?
4. Who is your best friend?
5. Can you tie your shoes?

Page 173

Asking Sentences

Directions: Write the first word of each asking sentence. Be sure to begin each question with a capital letter. End each question with a question mark.

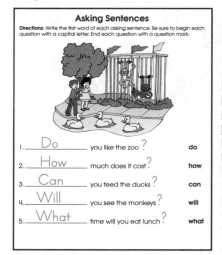

1. Do you like the zoo? do
2. How much does it cost? how
3. Can you feed the ducks? can
4. Will you see the monkeys? will
5. What time will you eat lunch? what

Page 174

Asking Sentences

Directions: Change each telling sentence into an asking sentence by moving the words. Put a question mark at the end of each question.

Example: He ate one cookie.

Is he eating one cookie?

1. She has two dogs.

Does she have two dogs?

2. Three balls can bounce.

Can three balls bounce?

3. One balloon is red.

Is one balloon red?

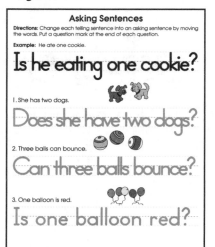

Page 175

Asking and Telling Sentences

Directions: Change the telling sentences into asking sentences. Change the asking sentences into telling sentences. Begin each one with a capital letter and end it with a period or a question mark.

Examples:

Is she eating three cookies?

She is eating three cookies.

He is bringing one truck.

Is he bringing one truck?

1. Is he painting two blue birds?

He is painting two bluebirds.

2. Did she find four apples?

She did find four apples.

3. She will be six on her birthday.

Will she be six on her birthday?

Page 176

Asking and Telling Sentences

Directions: Write the word that completes each sentence. Put a period at the end of the telling sentences and a question mark at the end of the asking sentences.

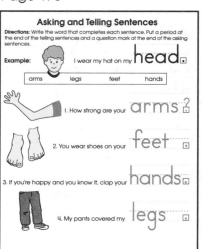

Example: I wear my hat on my head.

arms legs feet hands

1. How strong are your arms?
2. You wear shoes on your feet.
3. If you're happy and you know it, clap your hands.
4. My pants covered my legs.

Page 177

Asking and Telling Sentences

Directions: Write three telling sentences about the picture. Then write an asking sentence about the picture.

Answers may include:
Telling sentences:

1. The grass is green.
2. There are two trees.
3. The pool is pink.

Asking sentence:

Is the sky clear?

Page 178

Asking and Telling Sentences

Directions: Write two telling sentences and one asking sentence about this picture. Use the food, color, and animal words you know.

Answers may include:
Two telling sentences:

1. The cat is gray.
2. The egg is cracked.

One asking sentence:

Is the girl angry?

Page 179

Asking and Telling Sentences

Directions: Write two telling sentences and one asking sentence about this picture. Use the number words you know.

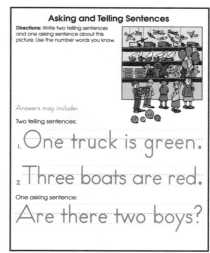

Answers may include:
Two telling sentences:

1. One truck is green.
2. Three boats are red.

One asking sentence:

Are there two boys?

Page 180

Following Directions

Directions: Look at the pictures. Follow the directions in each box.

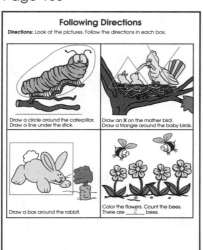

Draw a circle around the caterpillar. Draw a line under the stick.

Draw an **X** on the mother bird. Draw a triangle around the baby birds.

Draw a box around the rabbit.

Color the flowers. Count the bees. There are __2__ bees.

Page 181

Following Directions: Play Simon Says

Directions: Read how to play Simon Says. Then answer the questions.

Simon Says

Here is how to play Simon Says: One kid is Simon. Simon is the leader. Everyone must do what Simon says and does but only if the leader says, "Simon says" first. Let'try it. "Simon says, 'Pat your head.'" "Simon says, 'Pat your nose. Pat your toes.'"
Oops! Did you pat your toes? I did not say, "Simon says," first. If you patted your toes, you are out!

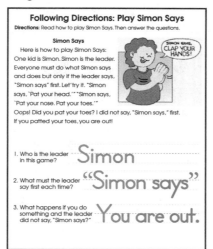

1. Who is the leader in this game? — Simon

2. What must the leader say first each time? — "Simon says"

3. What happens if you do something and the leader did not say, "Simon says?" — You are out.

Page 182

Following Directions: Play Simon Says

Directions: Read the sentences. If Simon tells you to do something, follow the directions. If Simon does not tell you to do something, go to the next sentence.

1. Simon says: Cross out all the numbers 2 through 9.
2. Simon says: Cross out the vowel that is in the word "sun."
3. Cross out the letter "B."
4. Cross out the vowels "A" and "E."
5. Simon says: Cross out the consonants in the word "cup."
6. Cross out the letter "Z."
7. Simon says: Cross out all the "K's."
8. Simon says: Read your message.

Answer: Great job!

C̶ G̶ U̶ T̶ P̶ R̶ U̶ C̶ P̶ E̶ K̶ C̶ P̶ A̶ B̶ K̶
G̶ T̶ P̶ U̶ P̶ J̶ C̶ G̶ P̶ O̶ K̶ G̶ P̶ B̶ U̶ P̶ K̶

Page 183

Following Directions: Play Simon Says

Directions: Read each sentence. Look at the picture next to it. Circle the picture if the person is playing Simon Says correctly.

1. Simon says, "Put your hands on your hips."

2. Simon says, "Stand on one leg."

3. Simon says, "Put your hands on your head."

4. Simon says, "Ride a bike."

5. Simon says, "Jump up and down."

6. Simon says, "Pet a dog."

7. Simon says, "Make a big smile."

Page 184

Following Directions

Directions: Draw a hat on each person. Read the sentences to know what kind of hat to draw.

1. The second girl is wearing a purple hat with feathers.

2. The boy next to the girl with the purple hat is wearing a red baseball hat.

3. The first boy is wearing a yellow knit hat.

4. The last boy is wearing a brown top hat.

5. The girl next to the boy with the red hat is wearing a blue straw hat.

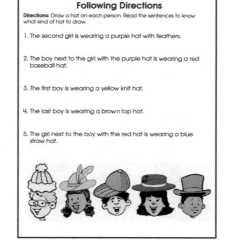

Page 185

Following Directions

Directions: Color the path the girl should take to go home. Use the sentences to help you.

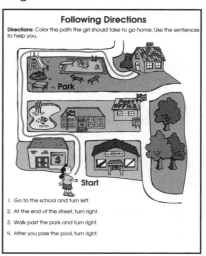

1. Go to the school and turn left.

2. At the end of the street, turn right.

3. Walk past the park and turn right.

4. After you pass the pool, turn right.

Page 186

Following Directions

Directions: Follow directions to complete the picture of the tiger.

1. Draw black stripes on the tiger's body and tail.
2. Color the tiger's tongue red.
3. Draw claws on the feet.
4. Draw a black nose and two black eyes on the tiger's face.
5. Color the rest of the tiger orange.
6. Draw tall, green grass for the tiger to sleep in.

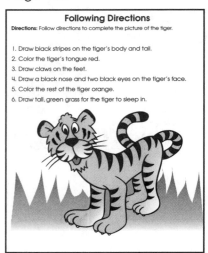

Page 187

Sequencing: Make an Ice-Cream Cone

Directions: Number the boxes in order to show how to make an ice-cream cone.

Page 188

Sequencing: Eating a Cone

What if a person never ate an ice-cream cone? Could you tell them how to eat it? Think about what you do when you eat an ice-cream cone.

Directions: Write directions to teach someone how to eat an ice-cream cone.

How to Eat an Ice-Cream Cone

1.
2.
3.
4.

Answers will vary.

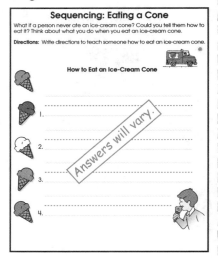

Page 189

Sequencing: Choosing a Hat

Directions: Write a number in each box to show the order of the story.

Page 190

Classifying

Directions: Draw a ☐ around objects that are food for the party. Draw a △ around the party guests. Draw a ◯ around the objects used for fun at the party.

ice cream · candy · games · tiger
noise makers · cake · garbage can · cat · hat
glasses · candle · bear · juice · balloons
giraffe · pig · potato chips · hippo

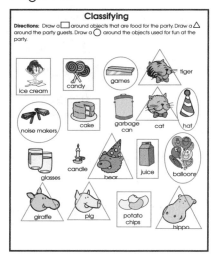

Page 191

Classifying: What Does Not Belong?

Directions: Draw an **X** on the picture that does not belong in each group.

fruit — apple · peach · corn · watermelon
wild animals — bear · kitten · gorilla · lion
pets — cat · fish · elephant · dog
flowers — grass · rose · daisy · tulip

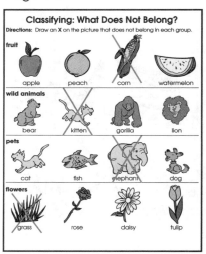

Page 192

Classifying

Directions: Color the meats and eggs brown. Color the fruits and vegetables green. Color the breads tan. Color the dairy foods (milk and cheese) yellow.

fish · bread · apple · cheese
crackers · carrot · orange · eggs
steaks · pear · milk · yogurt
ice cream · chicken · potato · pretzel

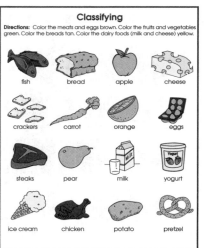

Page 193

Classifying: A Rainy Day

Directions: Read the story. Then circle the objects Jonathan needs to stay dry.

It is raining. Jonathan wants to play outdoors. What should he wear to stay dry? What should he carry to stay dry?

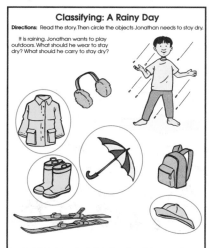

Developmental Skills for
Second Grade Reading Success

Parents and educators alike know that the School Specialty name ensures outstanding educational experience and content. Summer Link Reading was designed to help your child retain those skills learned during the past school year. With Summer Link Reading, your child will be ready to review and take on new material with confidence when he or she returns to school in the fall. The skills reviewed here will help your child be prepared for proficiency testing.

You can use this checklist to evaluate your child's progress. Place a check mark in the box if the appropriate skill has been mastered. If your child needs more work with a particular skill, place an "R" in the box and come back to it for review.

Reading Skills

Uses reading strategies:

- ☐ Uses pictures to tell a story
- ☐ Follows text from left to right
- ☐ Uses story content and pattern to predict

☐ Recalls main events in a story

☐ Recalls the conflict of a story

☐ Recalls the setting of a story

☐ Recalls the conclusion of a story

☐ Recalls or predicts a simple sequence of events

☐ Recognizes causes and effects of situations

Developmental Skills for Second Grade Reading Success

Language Arts

☐ Recognizes uppercase letters

☐ Recognizes lowercase letters

☐ Knows alphabetical sequence

☐ Knows consonant letter sounds

☐ Knows long and short vowel sounds

☐ Recognizes the beginning sounds of words

☐ Recognizes the ending sounds of words

☐ Recognizes the middle sounds of words

☐ Discriminates between rhyming and nonrhyming words

☐ Discriminates between antonyms and synonyms

☐ Correctly writes uppercase letters

☐ Correctly writes lowercase letters

☐ Uses memorized words when writing

☐ Uses knowledge of letter sounds to create words

☐ Makes illustrations to match writing

☐ Writing shows a sequence of events or clear ideas

☐ Engages in various writing forms: letters, books, etc.

☐ Recognizes complete and incomplete sentences

TEST PRACTICE

This page intentionally left blank.

Test Practice Table of Contents

Just for Parents

For All Students

Practice Test

Unit 1: Reading and Language Arts

Unit 2: Basic Skills

Unit 3: Mathematics

Final Test

What Are Standardized Achievement Tests?

Achievement tests measure what children know in particular subject areas such as reading, language arts, and mathematics. They do not measure your child's intelligence or ability to learn.

When tests are standardized, or *normed*, children's test results are compared with those of a specific group who have taken the test, usually at the same age or grade.

Standardized achievement tests measure what children around the country are learning. The test makers survey popular textbook series, as well as state curriculum frameworks and other professional sources, to determine what content is covered widely.

Because of variations in state frameworks and textbook series, as well as grade ranges on some test levels, the tests may cover some material that children have not yet learned. This is especially true if the test is offered early in the school year. However, test scores are compared to those of other children who take the test at the same time of year, so your child will not be at a disadvantage if his or her class has not covered specific material yet.

Different School Districts, Different Tests

There are many flexible options for districts when offering standardized tests. Many school districts choose not to give the full test battery, but select certain content and scoring options. For example, many schools may test only in the areas of reading and mathematics. Similarly, a state or district may use one test for certain grades and another test for other grades. These decisions are often based on the amount of time and money a district wishes to spend on test administration. Some states choose to develop their own statewide assessment tests.

On pages 209 and 210 you will find information about these five widely used standardized achievement tests:

- California Achievement Test (CAT)
- Terra Nova/CTBS
- Iowa Test of Basic Skills (ITBS)
- Stanford Achievement Test (SAT9)
- Metropolitan Achievement Test (MAT)

However, this book contains strategies and practice questions for use with a variety of tests. Even if your state does not give one of the five tests listed above, your child will benefit from doing the practice questions in this book. If you're unsure about which test your child takes, contact your local school district to find out which tests are given.

Types of Test Questions

Traditionally, standardized achievement tests have used only multiple-choice questions. Today, many tests may include constructed response (short answer) and extended response (essay) questions as well.

In addition, many tests include questions that tap students' higher-order thinking skills. Instead of simple recall questions, such as identifying a date in history, questions may require students to make comparisons and contrasts or analyze results, among other skills.

What the Tests Measure

These tests do not measure your child's level of intelligence, but they do show how well your child knows material that he or she has learned and that is

also covered on the tests. It's important to remember that some tests cover content that is not taught in your child's school or grade. In other instances, depending on when in the year the test is given, your child may not yet have covered the material.

If the test reports you receive show that your child needs improvement in one or more skill areas, you may want to seek help from your child's teacher and find out how you can work with your child to improve his or her skills.

California Achievement Test (CAT/5)

What Is the California Achievement Test?

The *California Achievement Test* is a standardized achievement test battery that is widely used with elementary through high school students.

Parts of the Test

The *CAT* includes tests in the following content areas:

Reading
* Word Analysis
* Vocabulary
* Comprehension

Spelling

Language Arts
* Language Mechanics
* Language Usage

Mathematics

Science

Social Studies

Your child may take some or all of these subtests if your district uses the *California Achievement Test*.

Terra Nova/CTBS (Comprehensive Tests of Basic Skills)

What Is the Terra Nova/CTBS?

The *Terra Nova/Comprehensive Tests of Basic Skills* is a standardized achievement test battery used in elementary through high school grades.

While many of the test questions on the *Terra Nova* are in the traditional multiple choice form, your child may take parts of the *Terra Nova* that include some open-ended questions (constructed-response items).

Parts of the Test

Your child may take some or all of the following subtests if your district uses the *Terra Nova/CTBS*:

Reading/Language Arts

Mathematics

Science

Social Studies

Supplementary tests include:
* Word Analysis
* Vocabulary
* Language Mechanics
* Spelling
* Mathematics Computation

Critical thinking skills may also be tested.

Iowa Test of Basic Skills (ITBS)

What Is the ITBS?

The *Iowa Test of Basic Skills* is a standardized achievement test battery used in elementary through high school grades.

Parts of the Test

Your child may take some or all of these subtests if your district uses the *ITBS*, also known as the *Iowa*:

Reading
- Vocabulary
- Reading Comprehension

Language Arts
- Spelling
- Capitalization
- Punctuation
- Usage and Expression

Math
- Concepts/Estimate
- Problems/Data Interpretation

Social Studies

Science

Sources of Information

Stanford Achievement Test (SAT9)

What Is the Stanford Achievement Test?

The *Stanford Achievement Test, Ninth Edition (SAT9)* is a standardized achievement test battery used in elementary through high school grades.

Note that the *Stanford Achievement Test (SAT9)* is a different test from the *SAT* used by high school students for college admissions.

While many of the test questions on the *SAT9* are in traditional multiple choice form, your child may take parts of *the SAT9* that include some open-ended questions (constructed-response items).

Parts of the Test

Your child may take some or all of these subtests if your district uses the *Stanford Achievement Test*:

Reading
- Vocabulary
- Reading Comprehension

Mathematics
- Problem Solving
- Procedures

Language Arts

Spelling

Study Skills

Listening
Critical thinking skills may also be tested.

Metropolitan Achievement Test (MAT7 and MAT8)

What Is the Metropolitan Achievement Test?

The *Metropolitan Achievement Test* is a standardized achievement test battery used in elementary through high school grades.

Parts of the Test

Your child may take some or all of these subtests if your district uses the *Metropolitan Achievement Test*:

Reading
- Vocabulary
- Reading Comprehension

Math
- Concepts and Problem Solving
- Computation

Language Arts
- Pre-writing
- Composing
- Editing

Science

Social Studies

Research Skills

Thinking Skills

Spelling

Statewide Assessments

Today the majority of states give statewide assessments. In some cases these tests are known as *high-stakes assessments*. This means that students must score at a certain level in order to be promoted. Some states use minimum competency or proficiency tests. Often these tests measure more basic skills than other types of statewide assessments.

Statewide assessments are generally linked to state curriculum frameworks. Frameworks provide a blueprint, or outline, to ensure that teachers are covering the same curriculum topics as other teachers in the same grade level in the state. In some states, standardized achievement tests (such as the five described in this book) are used in connection with statewide assessments.

When Statewide Assessments Are Given

Statewide assessments may not be given at every grade level. Generally, they are offered at one or more grades in elementary school, middle school, and high school. Many states test at grades 4, 8, and 10.

State-by-State Information

You can find information about statewide assessments and curriculum frameworks at your state Department of Education Web site. To find the address for your individual state, go to www.ed.gov, click on Topics A–Z, and then click on State Departments of Education. You will find a list of all the state departments of education, mailing addresses, and Web sites.

How to Help Your Child Prepare for Standardized Testing

Preparing All Year Round

Perhaps the most valuable way you can help your child prepare for standardized achievement tests is by providing enriching experiences. Keep in mind also that test results for younger children are not as reliable as for older students. If a child is hungry, tired, or upset, this may result in a poor test score. Here are some tips on how you can help your child do his or her best on standardized tests.

Read aloud with your child. Reading aloud helps develop vocabulary and fosters a positive attitude toward reading. Reading together is one of the most effective ways you can help your child succeed in school.

Share experiences. Baking cookies together, planting a garden, or making a map of your neighborhood are examples of activities that help build skills that are measured on the tests, such as sequencing and following directions.

Become informed about your state's testing procedures. Ask about or watch for announcements of meetings that explain about standardized tests and statewide assessments in your school district. Talk to your child's teacher about your child's individual performance on these state tests during a parent-teacher conference.

Help your child know what to expect. Read and discuss with your child the test-taking tips in this book. Your child can prepare by working through a couple of strategies a day so that no practice session takes too long.

Help your child with his or her regular school assignments. Set up a quiet study area for homework. Supply this area with pencils, paper, markers, a calculator, a ruler, a dictionary, scissors, glue, and so on. Check your child's homework and offer to help if he or she gets stuck. But remember, it's your child's homework, not yours. If you help too much, your child will not benefit from the activity.

Keep in regular contact with your child's teacher. Attend parent-teacher conferences, school functions, PTA or PTO meetings, and school board meetings. This will help you get to know the educators in your district and the families of your child's classmates.

Learn to use computers as an educational resource. If you do not have a computer and Internet access at home, try your local library.

Remember—simply getting your child comfortable with testing procedures and helping him or her know what to expect can improve test scores!

Getting Ready for the Big Day

There are lots of things you can do on or immediately before test day to improve your child's chances of testing success. What's more, these strategies will help your child prepare him-or herself for school tests, too, and promote general study skills that can last a lifetime.

Provide a good breakfast on test day. Instead of sugar cereal, which provides immediate but not long-term energy, have your child eat a breakfast with protein or complex carbohydrates, such as an egg, whole grain cereal or toast, or a banana-yogurt shake.

Promote a good night's sleep. A good night's sleep before the test is essential. Try not to overstress the importance of the test. This may cause your child to lose sleep because of anxiety. Doing some exercise after school and having a quiet evening routine will help your child sleep well the night before the test.

Assure your child that he or she is not expected to know all of the answers on the test. Explain that other children in higher grades may take the same test, and that the test may measure things your child has not yet learned in school. Help your child understand that you expect him or her to put forth a good effort—and that this is enough. Your child should not try to cram for these tests. Also avoid threats or bribes; these put undue pressure on children and may interfere with their best performance.

Keep the mood light and offer encouragement. To provide a break on test days, do something fun and special after school—take a walk around the neighborhood, play a game, read a favorite book, or prepare a special snack together. These activities keep your child's mood light—even if the testing sessions have been difficult—and show how much you appreciate your child's effort.

Taking Standardized Tests

What You Need to Know About Taking Tests

You can get better at taking tests. Here are some tips.

Do your schoolwork.
Study in school. Do your homework all the time. These things will help you in school and on any tests you take. Learn new things a little at a time. Then you will remember them better when you see them on a test.

Feel your best.
One way you can do your best on tests and in school is to make sure your body is ready. Get a good night's sleep. Eat a healthy breakfast.

One more thing: Wear comfortable clothes. You can also wear your lucky shirt or your favorite color on test day. It can't hurt. It may even make you feel better about the test.

Be ready for the test.
Do practice questions. Learn about the different kinds of questions. Books like this one will help you.

Follow the test directions.
Listen carefully to the directions your teacher gives. Read all instructions carefully. Watch out for words such as *not, none, never, all,* and *always*. These words can change the meaning of the directions. You may want to circle words like these. This will help you keep them in mind as you answer the questions.

Look carefully at each page before you start.
Do reading tests in a special order. First, read the directions. Read the questions next. This way you will know what to look for as you read. Then read the story. Last, read the story again quickly. Skim it to find the best answer.

On math tests, look at the labels on graphs and charts.
Think about what the graph or chart shows. You will often need to draw conclusions about the information to answer some questions.

Use your time wisely. Many tests have time limits. Look at the clock when the test starts. Figure out when you need to stop. When you begin, look over the whole thing. Do the easy parts first. Go back and do the hard parts last. Make sure you do not spend too much time on any one part. This way, if you run out of time, you still have completed much of the test.

Fill in the answer circles the right way. Fill in the whole circle. Make your pencil mark dark, but not so dark that it goes through the paper! Be sure you pick just one answer for each question. If you pick two answers, both will be marked as wrong.

Use context clues to figure out hard questions. You may come across a word or an idea you don't understand. First, try to say it in your own words. Then use context clues— the words in the sentences nearby— to help you figure out its meaning.

Sometimes it's good to guess. Here's what to do. Each question may have four or five answer choices. You may know that two answers are wrong, but you are not sure about the rest. Then make your best guess. If you are not sure about any of the answers, skip it. Do not guess. Tests like these take away extra points for wrong answers. So it is better to leave them blank.

Check your work. You may finish the test before the time is up. Then you can go back and check your answers. Make sure you answered each question you could. Also, make sure that you filled in only one answer circle for each question. Erase any extra marks on the page.

Finally—stay calm! Take time to relax before the test. One good way to relax is to get some exercise. Stretch, shake out your fingers, and wiggle your toes. Take a few slow, deep breaths. Then picture yourself doing a great job!

Skills Checklists

In which subjects do you need more practice? Find out. Use the checklists below. These are skills you should have mastered in Grade 1. Read each sentence. Is it true for you? Put a check next to it. Then look at the unchecked sentences. These are the skills you need to review.

Reading, Language Arts, and Writing: Grade 1

Reading

☐ I can find the main idea.

☐ I can note details.

☐ I can understand characters' feelings.

☐ I can figure out the author's purpose for writing.

☐ I use information from a story and what I already know to make inferences and draw conclusions.

☐ I can compare and contrast.

☐ I can find what happens first, next, and last.

☐ I can predict what will happen next in a story.

☐ I can choose the best title for a story.

Language Arts

I can identify and use different parts of speech.

☐ nouns or naming words

☐ plurals or nouns that name more than one

☐ verbs or action words

☐ adjectives or describing words

☐ pronouns

☐ I can tell the difference between a complete and an incomplete sentence.

☐ I can change a telling sentence to an asking sentence.

☐ I use end punctuation correctly.

☐ I use capital letters correctly.

Writing

Before I write

☐ I think about who will read my work.

☐ I think about my purpose for writing (to inform or entertain).

When I write a draft

☐ It has a main idea and supporting details.

☐ I use words and actions that tell about my characters.

☐ I use words that tell about the setting.

As I revise my work

☐ I check for spelling, capitalization, punctuation, and grammar mistakes.

☐ I take out parts that are not necessary.

☐ I add words and sentences to make my work more interesting.

☐ I neatly write or type my final copy.

☐ I include my name and a title on the finished work.

Word Analysis/Phonics

☐ I can find root words.

☐ I understand prefixes and suffixes.

I can match

☐ beginning sounds

☐ ending sounds

☐ vowel sounds

Vocabulary

☐ I can use context clues to figure out hard words.

☐ I know what synonyms are.

☐ I can find words with opposite meanings.

☐ I can read sight words.

☐ I can find written words from spoken definitions.

Mathematics: Grade 1

Numeration

❏ I can count to 100.

❏ I can count objects to 100.

❏ I can compare groups of objects.

❏ I can read numbers from 0 to 100.

❏ I can count on by 2s, 3s, 4s, 5s, and 10s.

❏ I can find the ones place and the tens place in a number and tell what that means.

Addition and Subtraction

❏ I know addition and subtraction facts to 18.

❏ I can add two-digit numbers with no regrouping.

❏ I write and solve number sentences.

Problem Solving

❑ When I do number problems, I read the directions carefully.

❑ When I do word problems, I read the problem carefully.

❑ I look for words that tell whether I must add or subtract to solve the problem.

Time, Measurement, Money, and Geometry

❑ I can use charts and graphs.

❑ I can tell time on both kinds of clocks.

❑ I can measure lengths.

❑ I understand how much coins are worth.

❑ I know the basic shapes.

❑ I can match shape patterns.

❑ I can find lines of symmetry.

Getting Ready All Year

You can do better in school and on tests if you know how to study and make good use of your time. Here are some tips.

Make it easy to get your homework done. Set up a place in which to do it each day. Choose a place that is quiet. Get the things you need, such as pencils, paper, and markers. Put them in your homework place.

Homework Log and Weekly Calendar Make your own homework log. Or copy the one on pages 222–223 of this book. Write down your homework each day. Also list other things you have to do, such as sports practice or music lessons. Then you won't forget easily.

Do your homework right away. Do it soon after you get home from school. Give yourself a lot of time. Then you won't be too tired to do it later on.

Get help if you need it. If you need help, just ask. Call a friend. Or ask a family member. If they cannot help you, ask your teacher the next day.

Figure out how you learn best. Some people learn best by listening, others by looking. Some learn best by doing something with their hands or moving around. Some children like to work in groups. And some are very happy working alone.

Think about your favorite parts of school. Are you good in art, mathematics, or maybe gym? Your favorite class maybe a clue to how you learn best. Try to figure it out. Then use it to study and learn better.

Practice, practice, practice! The best way to get better is by practicing a lot. You may have trouble in a school subject. Do some extra work in that subject. It can give you just the boost you need.

 # Homework Log
and Weekly Schedule

	MONDAY	TUESDAY	WEDNESDAY
MATHEMATICS			
READING			
LANGUAGE ARTS			
OTHER			

for the week of _____

THURSDAY	FRIDAY	SATURDAY/SUNDAY	
			MATHEMATICS
			READING
			LANGUAGE ARTS
			OTHER

What's Ahead in This Book?

Everyone in school has to take tests. This book will help you get ready for them. Ask a family member to help you.

The best way to get ready for tests is to do your best in school. You can also learn about the kinds of questions that will be on them. That is what this book is about. It will help you know what to do on the day of the test.

You will learn about the questions that will be on the test. You will get questions on which to practice. You will get hints for how to answer the questions.

In the last part of this book, there is a Practice Test and Final Test for Grade 1. These tests look like the ones you take in school. There is also a list of answers to help you check your answers.

If you practice, you will be all ready on test day.

Multiple Choice Questions

A multiple choice question has 3 or 4 answer choices.
You must choose the right answer.

EXAMPLE **Which word does *not* fit in this group?**

dog, cat, _____

○ hamster

○ goldfish

○ bike

Sometimes you will know the answer right away. Other times you won't. To answer multiple choice questions on a test, do the following:

• Always read or listen to the directions.

• Look at each answer first. Then mark which one you think is right.

• Answer easy questions first.

• Skip hard questions. Come back to them later. Circle the question to remember which ones you still need to do.

Testing It Out
Now look at the sample question more closely.

Think: Dogs and cats are both pets. I see the word *not*. I need a word that is not a kind of pet. Hamsters and goldfish are pets. I know that a bike is not a pet. I will choose bike.

Multiple Choice Practice

Directions: Find the word that means the same thing, or almost the same thing, as the underlined word. Fill in the circle next to your answer.

Directions: Find the word that rhymes with the underlined word. Fill in the circle next to your answer.

1 <u>delicious</u> pizza

○ boring

○ hungry

○ tasty

2 <u>below</u> the desk

○ above

○ behind

○ under

3 I am afraid of <u>mice</u>.

○ bears

○ rice

○ moose

4 I like to eat spaghetti <u>dinner</u>.

○ winner

○ supper

○ finger

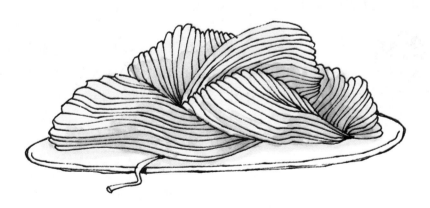

Fill-in-the-Blank Questions

On some tests you must find a word that is missing from a sentence.

EXAMPLE _____ **your teeth before you go to bed.**

- ○ Smile

- ○ Brush

- ○ Buy

To answer fill-in-the-blank questions:

- Try to think of the answer before you look at the choices.

- See if one of the choices matches your answer.

- Always check the other choices. There may be a better answer.

Testing It Out
Now look at the sample question above more closely.

Think: *Smile* reminds me of teeth. But it does not make sense. *Brush* seems right. I will look at all the choices. *Buy* starts with the same letter as *Brush*. But it does not make sense. I will mark *Brush*.

Fill-in-the-Blank Practice

Directions: Find the word that best completes the sentence. Fill in the circle next to your answer.

1 **The cereal is _____.**

○ in the bowl

○ at a movie

○ in the attic

2 **The _____ is full of apples.**

○ tall tree

○ blue sea

○ big building

3 **When I am thirsty, I _____.**

○ chop wood

○ sing songs

○ drink water

4 **We had cake at my birthday _____.**

○ hike

○ party

○ flower

5 **Be _____ not to touch the oven.**

○ careful

○ happy

○ silly

Oral Questions

On some tests you will listen to your teacher read a word. Then you will answer a question about the sounds. Ask an adult to read you the questions.

EXAMPLE **Which word starts with the same sound as *dish*?**

○ plate

○ door

○ bath

To answer oral questions:

• Listen to the directions.

• Say each answer to yourself. Listen to the sounds.

• Look at all the words. Then mark the one you think is correct.

Testing It Out
Now look at the sample question more closely.

Think: *Plate* means the same thing as *dish*. But it does not start with the same sound. *Door* starts with the same sound as *dish*. *Bath* does not start with the same sound. *Door* must be the right answer.

Oral Questions Practice

Directions: Listen to an adult say the word.
Fill in the circle next to the word that starts with same sound.

1 desk

    ○ chair   ○ bat   ○ den

Directions: Listen to an adult say the word. Fill in the circle next to the word that ends with same sound.

2 make

    ○ man   ○ nose   ○ rock

Directions: Listen to an adult say the word. Fill in the circle next to the word that rhymes.

3 find

    ○ left   ○ fun   ○ kind

Short Answer Questions

Some questions do not give you answers to choose from.
You must write short answers in your own words.

EXAMPLE

dog   cat   rabbit   worm

Which animal does not fit into the group?

_____

Why?

_____

When you write short answers to questions on a test:

- Read each question. Make sure you answer the question. Do not write other things about the words or pictures.

- Your answer should be short. But make sure you answer the whole question.

- Write complete sentences.

Testing It Out

Now look at the sample question more closely.

Think: Dogs, cats, and rabbits have four legs and fur. But worms do not have legs or fur. So *worm* is the answer.

Which animal does not fit into the group?
<u>The worm does not fit into the group.</u>

Why?
<u>The other animals have four legs and fur. A worm does not.</u>

Short Answer Practice

Directions: Read the story. Then answer the questions.

Every Sunday I go with my dad to play basketball in the park. He teaches me how to dribble, pass, even slam-dunk! Sometimes he has to lift me up to reach the net. He says I will be a great player when I get taller. Sunday is my favorite day of the week.

1 **Why is Sunday the author's favorite day of the week?**

_____

_____

2 **How do you think the author feels about her father? Why?**

_____

_____

Directions: Look at the pictures to decide which one does not belong. Write your answers on the lines.

3

cup   plate   book

Which picture does not belong?

_____

Why?

_____

Choosing a Picture
to Answer a Question

Sometimes your teacher will read you a story and ask you a question about it. You will choose the picture that best answers the question. Ask an adult to read this story to you.

EXAMPLE Carly and Mike were best friends. One day they were playing hide and seek in Mike's back yard. Carly could not find Mike anywhere. Carly gave up and went into their tree house. She was very surprised when Mike popped out and said "boo!"

Where was Mike hiding?

   ○   ○   ○

When you choose a picture to answer a question on a test:

• Listen to the story carefully.

• Try to imagine what is happening. Choose the picture that is closest to what you imagine.

• Mark your answer as soon as you know which one is right. Then get ready for the next question.

• Change your answer only if you are sure it is wrong and another one is right.

Testing It Out

Now look at the sample question more closely. Where was Mike hiding?

Think: Mike did not hide *behind* a tree in the story. He did not hide *under* a bed. They were playing in the back yard. Mike was hiding in a tree house. The third picture is right.

Choosing a Picture
to Answer a Question Practice

Directions: Listen to the story. Then choose the picture that best answers the question.

Wendy was Tanya's baby sister. Wendy wanted to do everything Tanya did. Tanya was going to eat the last piece of cake. Wendy wanted a piece too. Tanya got an idea. She cut the piece of cake in half. They ate their snack together.

1 Which picture shows Wendy?

◯   ◯   ◯

2 What did Wendy want to eat?

◯   ◯   ◯

Math Questions

On some tests, you will have to answer math questions. Some of these questions will tell a story or show pictures.

EXAMPLE

Look at the picture. Which number sentence shows how many treats there are in all?

1 + 2 + 1 ○

4 + 6 ○

3 + 2 + 1 ○

When you answer math questions on a test:

• Look at the picture. Read all the choices. Then mark your answer.

• Look for important words and numbers.

• Draw pictures or write numbers on scratch paper.

• Look for clue words like *in all, more, less, left,* and *equal.*

Testing It Out

Look at the sample question more closely.

Think: I see 3 groups of treats. The number sentence should have 3 numbers. The first sentence has 3 numbers. But it does not match the pictures. The next sentence only has 2 numbers. They are also too big. The last sentence matches the picture. There are 3 cookies, 2 lollipops, and 1 candy bar.

Summer Link Super Edition Grade 2

Math Questions Practice

Directions: Fill in the circle next to the answer that matches the picture.

1

○ 39 cents

○ 40 cents

○ 50 cents

2

○ 13 books

○ 11 books

○ 14 books

Directions: Use scratch paper to work out your answer.
Then fill in the circle next to the right number.

3

26
+ 7

○ 33

○ 36

○ 39

4

11
21
+ 32

○ 34

○ 54

○ 64

Using a Graph

You will have to read a graph to answer some questions.

EXAMPLE

Who read the same amount of books?

○ Barbara and Tom

○ Sue and Barbara

○ Sammy and Sue

When answering graph questions:

• Read the question carefully.

• Look for clue words such as *most, least, same, more*, and *less*.

• You don't always need to count. Try to see how much of each column or row is filled in.

Testing It Out

Now look at the sample question more closely.

Think: Barbara read 2 books and Tom only read 1. Sue read 2 books and Barbara read 2 books. That is the same number. Sammy read 3 books and Sue read 2. The answer is Sue and Barbara.

Using a Graph Practice

Directions: The graph shows how many children get to school by bus, car, train, bike, and walking. Look at the graph. Then fill in the circle next to your answer.

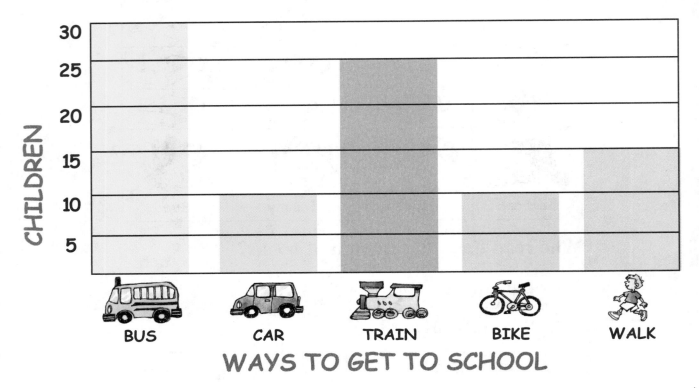

WAYS TO GET TO SCHOOL

1 **How do most children get to school?**

○ Bus

○ Car

○ Train

○ Bike

○ Walk

2 **How many children walk to school?**

○ 10

○ 15

○ 20

3 **Do more children ride in cars or on the train?**

○ Car

○ Train

Writing

On some tests you will have to write a long answer to a question. The question is called a writing prompt. Sometimes you may have to write a paragraph or a story.

EXAMPLE **Think of one thing that you do outside that you enjoy. Tell what you enjoy doing outside and why.**

When answering writing prompts:

• Write about something you know.

• Read the prompt carefully. Answer every part of the question.

• Plan your time. Leave enough time to check for spelling, punctuation, and grammar mistakes when you are finished.

Testing It Out

Look at the sample prompt more closely.

 **Think:** I want to write about something I really like to do. Let's see, what is my favorite thing to do? I like to play drums. But I do not do that outside. What is my favorite thing to do outside? I love to climb trees. I am a very good climber.

When I am outside, I like to climb trees. I know how to climb every tree in my backyard. I like climbing trees because when I get to the top, I can see down our whole street. Sometimes I see my friends and wave to them. Sometimes I feel like a bird looking down from the sky. Climbing trees makes me happy.

Writing Practice

Directions: Think of one thing you want to learn to do. What is it? Why do you want to learn how to do it? How can you learn it? Write your answers on the lines.

_____

_____

_____

_____

_____

_____

_____

_____

_____

_____

_____

_____

_____

_____

_____

_____

Grade 1 Introduction
to Practice Test and Final Test

On page 243, you will find Grade 1 Practice Test. On page 279, you will find Grade 1 Final Test. These tests will give you a chance to put the tips you have learned to work. It will also give you an idea about what skills you need to review to be ready for Grade 2.

Here are some things to remember as you take these tests:

- Read and listen carefully to all the directions.

- Be sure you understand all the directions before you begin.

- Ask an adult questions about the directions if you do not understand them.

- Work as quickly as you can during each test.

- Using a pencil, make sure to fill in only one little answer circle for each question. Don't mark outside the circle. If you change an answer, be sure to erase your first mark completely.

- If you're not sure about an answer, you can guess.

- Use the tips you have learned whenever you can.

- It is OK to be a little nervous. You may even do better.

- When you complete all the lessons in this book, you will be on your way to test success!

Grade 1 Table of Contents

Reading and Language Arts

Lesson 1 Story Reading

Directions: Find the words that fit best.

SAMPLE A **The toast is _____.**

on the dish   playing ball   in the closet

○   ○   ○

Directions: Listen to the story: Jonathan Harrison Turtle was in quite a fix. He had been taking his daily walk, when suddenly an owl had flown down and landed on his head.

SAMPLE B **Which picture shows what happened to the turtle?**

The turtle met   The turtle was   The owl was
a rabbit.   on the owl.   on the turtle.

○   ○   ○

Listen carefully to the directions.

Think about what you are supposed to do.

Look at each answer before marking the one you think is right.

GO

Name _____

Directions: Listen to the story: Carol wanted to ride her bike with her friend, Ramon. They would ride up the street to the playground. When she went to get her bike, Carol saw it had a flat tire.

1   **Which picture shows what was wrong with Carol's bike?**

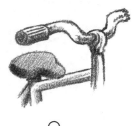      

   ○   ○   ○

2   **Find the picture that shows where Ramon and Carol wanted to go.**

   ○   ○   ○

3   **Find the sentence that tells how Carol probably felt when she saw her bike.**

   She was happy.   She was sad.   She didn't care.

       ○   ○   ○

Listen to the rest of the story: Carol told her big brother about the tire. He said he could fix it right away. He fixed the tire, and Carol could ride with her friend.

4   **Mark the circle under the words that tell what this story was mostly about.**

   going for a ride   fixing a bike   going to the playground

       ○   ○   ○

GO

Directions: Find the word that has the same beginning sound as <u>street</u>.

5   strong   teeth   horse

   ○   ○   ○

_____

Directions: Find the word that has the same beginning sound as <u>flat</u>.

6   tall   sat   fly

   ○   ○   ○

_____

Directions: Find the word that has the same middle sound as <u>ride</u>.

7   miss   line   hair

   ○   ○   ○

_____

Directions: Find the word that has the same middle sound as <u>get</u>.

8   ten   here   real

   ○   ○   ○

Directions: Many people in every neighborhood have pets. This story is about a boy and his pet. Read the story, then do numbers 9–12.

My dog's name is Nick. He is big and has long, brown hair. He likes to chase a ball. If I throw a ball, he catches it in his mouth. Brings it back to me. When I'm at school, Nick waits for me. He is standing near the door when I get home. He jumps up and licks my face. Then we go outside for a walk.

Francisco

GO

9   **What does Nick look like?**

He has long,   He is white   He is small with
brown hair.   with spots.   curly hair.

    ○   ○   ○

---

10   **Where is Nick when Francisco gets home?**

  ○   in the kitchen

  ○   on the bed

  ○   by the door

---

11   **If Francisco throws a stick, Nick will probably**

  ○   catch a ball.

  ○   bring it back.

  ○   lick his face.

GO

12 **Which of these is the best name for the story?**

- ○ My Dog Nick
- ○ Chasing a Ball
- ○ Walking the Dog

---

13 **This is Nick's ball.**

- ○ Is this Nick's ball?
- ○ Nick's ball is this?
- ○ Ball is this Nick's

---

14 <u>**Brings it back to me**</u> **is not a complete sentence. What should Francisco add to make it a complete sentence?**

_____ **brings it back to me.**

- ○ They
- ○ I
- ○ He

GO

15 **I take care of the dog.**
I walk the dog.

_____ .

- ○ I go to school.
- ○ I wash the dog.
- ○ I read a book.

---

16 **I am having a snack.**
I eat an apple.

_____ .

- ○ Mother is at work.
- ○ I like to go swimming.
- ○ Then I drink some milk.

STOP

Lesson 2 Reading a Poem

Directions: Listen to the poem. The kitten curled up on my lap. Pretty soon, it took a nap.

Which picture shows who took a nap?

○   ○   ○

Which word has the same beginning sound as <u>pull</u>?

pick   drip   desk

○   ○   ○

Think about the poem while you listen to it.

Mark your answer as soon as you know which one is right.

Change your answer only if you are sure it is wrong.

GO

Directions: Listen to the poem.   In the same house whose color is blue
Are lots of toy animals in Marilyn's zoo.

1   **Find the picture that shows where the zoo is.**

○   ○   ○

---

2   **Find the picture that shows which might be in the zoo.**

○   ○   ○

Listen to the next part of the poem.
    Some are small like Reggie Raccoon,
    But others are huge, like Betty Baboon.

3   **Find the picture that shows what Reggie is.**

○   ○   ○

GO

4 **Which picture shows Marilyn with Betty Baboon?**

○   ○   ○

Listen to the last part of the poem: Marilyn's bedroom is home to the zoo,
If you ever visit, she'll show it to you.

5 **Find the picture that shows where Marilyn keeps her animals.**

○   ○   ○

---

6 **Find the picture that shows what Marilyn would want to do first if someone visited her.**

○   ○   ○

GO

Directions: Find the word that has the same beginning sound as <u>large</u>.

7

leaf   arm   hill

○   ○   ○

Directions: Find the word that has the same beginning sound as <u>golf</u>.

8

fox   tall   gone

○   ○   ○

Directions: Find the word that has the same middle sound as <u>hat</u>.

9

bag   buy   bit

○   ○   ○

Directions: Find the word that has the same middle sound as <u>wet</u>.

10

room   rest   roll

○   ○   ○

STOP

Name _____

Lesson 3 Writing

Directions: Read the paragraph of information.

Cats are mammals. They have soft fur and long tails. Many cats live with people. These cats eat cat food. Wild cats may eat birds, bugs, or garbage. Cats meow when they are hungry. They purr when they are happy.

Directions: Think of an animal. Write a paragraph about it. Answer these questions:

- **How does the animal look?**

- **Where does it live?**

- **What does it eat?**

- **What are some of the things it does?**

_____

_____

_____

_____

_____

_____

GO

Name _____

Directions: Read the sentences that tell how to feed a hamster.

How to Feed a Hamster

Step 1. Get one scoop of food.

Step 2. Open the hamster's cage.

Step 3. Fill its bowl with food.

Step 4. Close the cage.

Directions: Think of something you can do or make. Write how-to sentences on the numbered lines below.

How to _____

Step 1 _____

_____

Step 2 _____

_____

Step 3 _____

_____

Step 4 _____

_____

STOP

Lesson 4 Review

Directions: Find the word that has the same beginning sound as <u>easy</u>.

 SAMPLE A

end	eat	ask
○	○	○

Directions: Find the word that has the same middle sound as <u>book</u>.

1

face	foot	find
○	○	○

2 The toy is on the bed.

  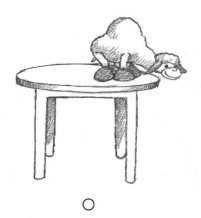

○	○	○

3 The door is open.

  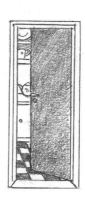

○	○	○

GO

Name _____

Directions: Listen to the story. Steven and his little sister were playing in the yard. They saw a bird land on the fence beside the house.

4 **Who was with Steven?**

 ○

 ○

 ○

5 **Where did the bird land?**

 ○

 ○

 ○

6 **Where were they playing?**

They were in the yard. ○

They were in school. ○

They were on the steps. ○

Directions: Listen to the story. The bird flew to the ground and picked up some dead grass. Then it flew into a tree. Steven said that the bird was building a nest.

7 **What is the story mostly about?**

two friends ○

playing a game ○

what a bird did ○

GO

Summer Link Super Edition Grade 2

Directions: For numbers 8 and 9, choose the correct end mark.

8   Dear Grandmother _____

   .   ,   ?
   ○   ○   ○

9   Thank you for the gift _____

   ?   ,   .
   ○   ○   ○

Directions: For numbers 10 and 11, mark the part of the sentence that needs a capital letter.

10   the coat | keeps me | very warm.
   ○   ○   ○

11   With | much love, | chris
   ○   ○   ○

Directions: Read the paragraph that describes a special day.

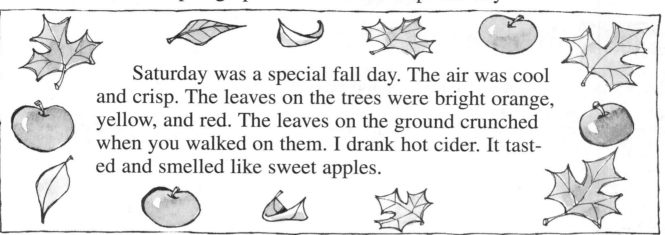

> Saturday was a special fall day. The air was cool and crisp. The leaves on the trees were bright orange, yellow, and red. The leaves on the ground crunched when you walked on them. I drank hot cider. It tasted and smelled like sweet apples.

Directions: Think about a special day. Write words in the web that describe your day.

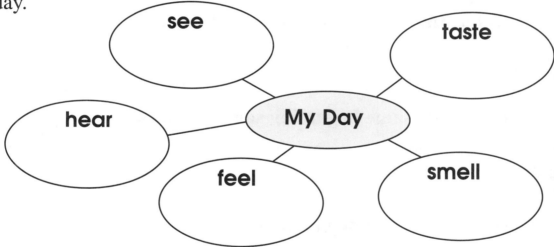

see

taste

hear

My Day

feel

smell

Directions: Write a paragraph that describes your special day. Use the ideas in your web.

_____

_____

_____

_____

STOP

Basic Skills

Lesson 1 Word Analysis

Directions: Which word has the same beginning sound as <u>bell</u>?

SAMPLE A

hill   boat   rest   cab
○   ○   ○   ○

TIPS Say each answer to yourself.
Listen for the beginning sound.

---

1 **Which word has the same beginning sound as <u>new</u>?**

when   tent   neat   shoe
○   ○   ○   ○

---

2 **Which word has the same beginning sound as <u>dark</u>?**

desk   park   sad   warm
○   ○   ○   ○

---

3 **Which word has the same beginning sound as <u>friend</u>?**

cry   trip   from
○   ○   ○

---

4 **Which word has the same beginning sound as <u>play</u>?**

please   stay   chain
○   ○   ○

---

5 **Which word has the same beginning sound as <u>skin</u>?**

clown   skip   slow
○   ○   ○

GO

Directions: Which word has the same ending sound as <u>far</u>?

SAMPLE B

fun	off	ran	her
○	○	○	○

Say each answer to yourself.
Listen for the ending sound.

6 **Which word has the same ending sound as <u>pin</u>?**

trap	can	nose	pet
○	○	○	○

7 **Which word has the same ending sound as <u>hit</u>?**

not	hear	win	dish
○	○	○	○

8 **Which word has the same ending sound as <u>have</u>?**

wish	head	van	love
○	○	○	○

9 **Which word has the same ending sound as <u>want</u>?**

wind	sent	both
○	○	○

10 **Which word has the same ending sound as <u>dirt</u>?**

learn	bird	heart
○	○	○

GO

Directions: Which word has the same middle sound as <u>cup</u>?

 SAMPLE C

turn   must   shout   hurt
○   ○   ○   ○

 Say each answer to yourself.
Listen for the middle sound.

11   **Which word has the same middle sound as <u>peach</u>?**

quiet   push   last   need
○   ○   ○   ○

12   **Which word has the same middle sound as <u>plane</u>?**

cake   rag   pants   mark
○   ○   ○   ○

13   **Which word has the same middle sound as <u>block</u>?**

voice   should   sock   roof
○   ○   ○   ○

14   **Which word has the same beginning sound as <u>eagle</u>?**

ant   and   end   eat
○   ○   ○   ○

STOP

Lesson 2 Vocabulary

Directions: Find the word that means <u>big</u>.

SAMPLE A

funny   cool   large   empty
  ○   ○   ○   ○

TIPS   Think about the definition.
           Choose the best answer.

1 **Find the word that means twelve months.**

yard   year   pail   mile
  ○   ○   ○   ○

---

2 **Find the word that means a kind of fruit.**

tree   bread   milk   orange
  ○   ○   ○   ○

---

3 **Find the word that means a place where people live.**

house   chair   roof   tree
  ○   ○   ○   ○

---

4 **Find the word that means something made of wood.**

dress   glove   brick   log
  ○   ○   ○   ○

---

5 **Find the word that means something that makes honey.**

fish   bird   bee   cow
  ○   ○   ○   ○

GO

Directions: Which answer means about the same as the underlined word?

SAMPLE **B**   <u>choose</u> them

- ○ hear
- ○ help
- ○ see
- ○ pick

SAMPLE **C**   was <u>awful</u>

- ○ bad
- ○ old
- ○ lazy
- ○ near

Directions: For numbers 6–11, choose the answer that means about the same as the underlined word.

6 <u>nap</u> now
- ○ race
- ○ sleep
- ○ stand
- ○ jump

7 be <u>speedy</u>
- ○ able
- ○ heavy
- ○ fast
- ○ better

8 <u>beneath</u> it
- ○ under
- ○ around
- ○ with
- ○ inside

9 will <u>enjoy</u>
- ○ miss
- ○ catch
- ○ like
- ○ dive

10 big <u>rock</u>
- ○ desk
- ○ stone
- ○ room
- ○ cliff

11 can <u>wash</u>
- ○ drink
- ○ float
- ○ hide
- ○ clean

GO

Directions: Which answer choice fits best in the blank?

SAMPLE
D   **The _____ deer was shy. It stood beside its mother.**

- ○ young   ○ brave
- ○ fast   ○ tall

Try each answer in the blank.

Directions: For numbers 12–17, find the word that best fits in the blank.

12 **We must _____ soon or we will be late.**

- ○ play   ○ start
- ○ call   ○ study

13 **Put the ladder _____ the wall so I can climb up.**

- ○ inside   ○ along
- ○ against   ○ below

14 **Put the food on the _____ and then serve it.**

- ○ dishes   ○ floor
- ○ stove   ○ chairs

15 **The _____ was bright. It was easy to see even though it was night.**

- ○ moon   ○ cloud
- ○ sun   ○ fog

16 **Helena _____ her room blue and white.**

- ○ cleaned   ○ fixed
- ○ slept   ○ painted

17 **The cat's claws are _____ , so be careful when you play with it.**

- ○ soft   ○ sharp
- ○ furry   ○ nice

STOP

Lesson 3 Computation

Directions: Add to find the answer.

 SAMPLE A

$$\begin{array}{r} 3 \\ + 2 \\ \hline \end{array}$$

○ 1
○ 5
○ 6
○ 32

1

$7 + 3 =$

○ 4
○ 21
○ 10
○ 37

2

$$\begin{array}{r} 4 \\ 1 \\ + 2 \\ \hline \end{array}$$

○ 7
○ 5
○ 3
○ 8

3

$10 + 30 =$

○ 20
○ 40
○ 13
○ 31

Directions: Subtract to find the answer.

SAMPLE B

$$\begin{array}{r} 5 \\ - 1 \\ \hline \end{array}$$

○ 4
○ 6
○ 3
○ 15

4

$$\begin{array}{r} 8 \\ - 2 \\ \hline \end{array}$$

○ 11
○ 6
○ 28
○ 10

5

$66¢ - 5¢ =$

○ 16¢
○ 61¢
○ 51¢
○ 65¢

6

$$\begin{array}{r} 14 \\ - 7 \\ \hline \end{array}$$

○ 21
○ 6
○ 7
○ 9

Pay attention to the operation sign so you know what to do.

STOP

Lesson 4 Review

Directions: Find the word that has the same beginning sound as will.

SAMPLE A

saw ○   new ○   done ○   won ○

1 **Find the word that has the same beginning sound as four.**

corn ○   dark ○   fork ○   lift ○

2 **Find the word that has the same beginning sound as map.**

more ○   home ○   rest ○   smooth ○

3 **Find the word that has the same beginning sound as speak.**

dress ○   spill ○   slip ○

4 **Find the word that has the same ending sound as leg.**

rug ○   gone ○   rich ○   grab ○

5 **Find the word that has the same ending sound as bread.**

dust ○   end ○   lose ○   sled ○

6 **Find the word that has the same ending sound as wild.**

hand ○   hold ○   toast ○

GO

Name _____

Directions: Which word has the same middle sound as <u>bird</u>?

SAMPLE
B

like   heard   noise   miss
○   ○   ○   ○

---

7 **Find the word that has the same middle sound as <u>cow</u>.**

hope   roar   round   pop
○   ○   ○   ○

---

8 **Find the word that has the same middle sound as <u>tent</u>.**

rest   team   seem   they
○   ○   ○   ○

---

9 **Find the word that has the same middle sound as <u>rain</u>.**

load   that   bread   game
○   ○   ○   ○

---

10 **Find the word that has the same middle sound as <u>fruit</u>.**

root   hope   boat   cow
○   ○   ○   ○

---

11 **Find the word that has the same middle sound as <u>kite</u>.**

fair   list   have   five
○   ○   ○   ○

---

12 **Find the word that has the same middle sound as <u>can</u>.**

bend   hand   what   don't
○   ○   ○   ○

GO

Directions: Find the word that means something that you read.

SAMPLE
C

snack   book   seat   sound

○   ○   ○   ○

13 **Which word means a small city?**

road   hill   house   town

○   ○   ○   ○

14 **Which word means a body of water?**

lake   field   tree   cave

○   ○   ○   ○

Directions: Find the word that means about the same as the underlined word.

15 <u>search</u> for

- ○ race
- ○ jump
- ○ look
- ○ write

16 large <u>boat</u>

- ○ wagon
- ○ balloon
- ○ cart
- ○ ship

17 will <u>listen</u>

- ○ hear
- ○ taste
- ○ find
- ○ sell

18 <u>wet</u> cloth

- ○ damp
- ○ small
- ○ soft
- ○ warm

GO

Directions: Which answer choice fits best in the blank?

Directions: Which answer solves the problem?

SAMPLE D
The ice was so _____ . We couldn't walk on it.

○ safe ○ thick
○ thin ○ cold

SAMPLE E

$$8 + 4$$

○ 12
○ 4
○ 48
○ 84

19 The box was so heavy it took two of us to _____ it.

○ lift
○ see
○ find

20 The oven is hot. Now we can _____ the cookies.

○ taste
○ eat
○ buy
○ bake

21 Put your coat in the _____ and then close the door.

○ garden
○ box
○ closet

22

$$11¢ + 61¢ =$$

○ 50¢
○ 52¢
○ 72¢
○ 73¢

23

$$9 + 9 =$$

○ 99
○ 0
○ 19
○ 18

24

$$44¢ - 24¢$$

○ 68¢
○ 20¢
○ 60¢
○ 28¢

25

$$62 - 4 =$$

○ 52
○ 66
○ 12
○ 58

STOP

Mathematics

Lesson 1 Mathematics Skills

Directions: Rudy has one dollar. He used it to buy a book. After he paid for the book, he got 3 pennies back.

 Which book did he buy?

$.93 $.97 $.87 $.77

○   ○   ○   ○

Listen carefully. Think about the question while you look at the answer choices.

Listen for key words and numbers.

As soon as you know which answer is right, mark it and get ready for the next item.

If you aren't sure which answer is correct, take your best guess.

GO

Name _____

Tammy's mother wanted to serve fruit in addition to cookies and cake at a party. She asked each child to draw a picture of the fruit he or she liked best.

1 **How many children liked apples best?**

     1   2   3   4

     ○   ○   ○   ○

GO

2 **Which fruit got the most votes?**

Apples   Bananas   Grapes   Oranges

○   ○   ○   ○

---

3 **Which fruit got two more votes than pears?**

Strawberries   Grapes   Apples   Bananas

○   ○   ○   ○

4 **Which child is number 6 in line?**

○   ○   ○   ○

---

5 **Tommy's party started at 2:00. If the party lasted two and one-half hours, what time did the party end?**

○   ○   ○   ○

6

Directions: Find the round clock that tells the same time.

○   ○   ○   ○

Directions: Find the object that is as tall as 3 postage stamps.

7

   ○   ○   ○   ○

STOP

Lesson 2 Review

Math Partners

Directions: How many blocks are in this tower?

SAMPLE A

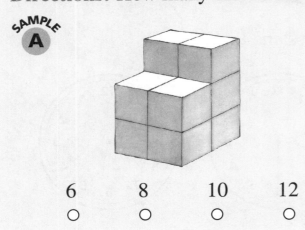

6	8	10	12
○	○	○	○

1 How many candies are there in all?

36	306	603	63
○	○	○	○

2 How much money is shown here?

3¢	12¢	21¢	16¢
○	○	○	○

GO

Name _____

Directions: Look at the pattern in the box. Mark the answer that has the same kind of pattern.

3

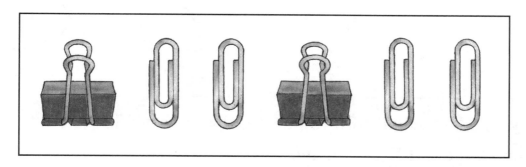

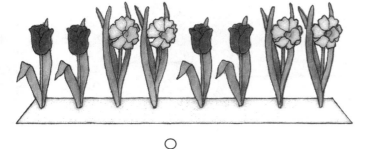

○

○

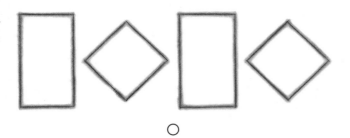

○

○

Directions: Find the picture that shows a group of 8.

4

○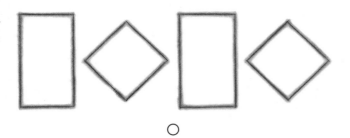

○

○

○

Name _____

5 Which number is 67?

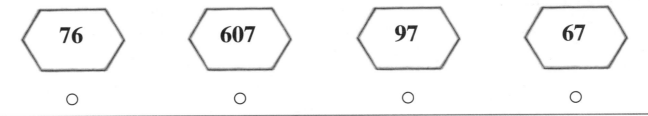

○   ○   ○   ○

---

6 Ricky's father asked him to draw a triangle inside a circle.

Which shape did Ricky draw?

○   ○   ○   ○

7

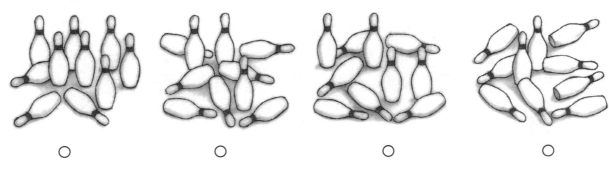

How many ducks were left standing on the edge?

5   6   7   8
○   ○   ○   ○

---

8 Ricky knocked down seven pins with his first ball.

Which picture shows how many were left standing?

○   ○   ○   ○

STOP

Reading and Language Arts

 SAMPLE A

Flowers are pretty. They are also food for some animals like bees, other insects, and birds.

Who gets food from a flower?

a bee	a snake	a fish
○	○	○

Directions: Brenda is a butterfly who has a problem. Winter is coming and she is getting cold. Read the story about Brenda, then do numbers 1–5.

Brenda was cold. She had never been cold before. She lived in a sunny place that was usually warm. Brenda did not like being cold.

Brenda's friend, Ralph, saw that she was sad. "Why the long face?" asked Ralph.

"I'm cold," answered Brenda, "and I don't know what to do."

GO

Ralph grinned at Brenda. He answered, "My mother told me what to do. She said we should follow the other butterflies and fly south. It's warm there all the time."

Brenda and Ralph saw some other butterflies. They followed them south, and soon Brenda was happy again.

1 **Ralph says that Brenda has a "long face."**

He is saying that

○   Brenda's face is long.

○   Brenda looks sad.

○   Brenda is a very tall butterfly.

GO

2 In the story,

| Ralph grinned at Brenda. |

What does this mean?

○ He was cold, too.

○ He didn't know what to do.

○ He smiled at her.

3 **Why was Brenda happy at the end of the story?**

○ She knows winter is coming.

○ She was warm again.

○ Ralph showed her how to fly.

4 **In which direction do Ralph and Brenda fly?**

○ north

○ west

○ south

5 **Birds sometimes go south for the winter. How else are they like butterflies?**

○ They both fly.

○ They both swim.

○ They both have six legs.

GO

Directions: For numbers 6 and 7, find the word that fits best in each blank in the story.

> While they were going south, Brenda and Ralph flew over a __(6)__ . They saw some __(7)__ in it and people swimming.

6 ○ field
    ○ lake
    ○ farm

7 ○ cars
    ○ trucks
    ○ boats

Directions: Find the word that can take the place of Brenda and Ralph.

8 Some children saw <u>Brenda and Ralph</u>.

    ○ them
    ○ they
    ○ it

Directions: Find the sentence that is written correctly.

9 ○ Many miles with their friends.
    ○ They flew to a warm place.
    ○ Tasty flowers all around.

STOP

Name _____

Directions: Read the letter that one girl wrote to a friend. Then think about what you would say in a friendly letter. Write it on the lines below.

May 5, 2002

Dear Mia,
    I won my race at field day last week. I got a blue ribbon.

          Your friend,
          Liz

Directions: Think about what you would say in a friendly letter. Write it on the lines below.

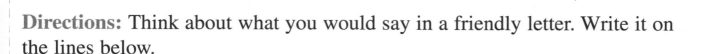

_____

_____

_____

_____

_____

_____

Directions: Read the story one child wrote.

> Chick thought Duck was mad at him. Duck was sitting by himself. Chick asked Duck what was wrong. Chick gave him treats and toys. At last Duck explained. Duck was not mad. He just wanted to be alone for a while. He and Chick were still best friends.

Directions: Think about a story you would like to write. Fill in the story map.

Beginning [ ]

⬇

Middle [ ]

⬇

Ending [ ]

Directions: Use your story map to write your story.

_____

_____

_____

_____

_____

_____

STOP

Basic Skills

Directions: Find the word that has the same beginning sound as joke.

SAMPLE A

pay   jump   mop   funny
○   ○   ○   ○

---

1   Which word has the same beginning sound as pork?

dust   late   pool   clap
○   ○   ○   ○

---

2   Which word has the same beginning sound as van?

toast   move   near   vote
○   ○   ○   ○

---

3   Which word has the same beginning sound as chest?

choose   touch   song   these
○   ○   ○   ○

---

4   Which word has the same ending sound as knob?

coat   lunch   dear   club
○   ○   ○   ○

---

5   Which word has the same ending sound as stew?

net   wheel   now   give
○   ○   ○   ○

---

6   Which word has the same ending sound as third?

hard   land   barn   dark
○   ○   ○   ○

GO

Name _____

Directions: Find the word that has the same middle sound as <u>corn</u>?

 SAMPLE **B**

      bone   rose   fort   loud

       ○   ○   ○   ○

---

7   **Which word has the same middle sound as <u>watch</u>?**

      lock   lead   home   roast

       ○   ○   ○   ○

---

8   **Which word has the same middle sound as <u>ring</u>?**

      find   chair   rise   sink

       ○   ○   ○   ○

---

9   **Which word has the same middle sound as <u>bump</u>?**

  young   four   show   coast

   ○   ○   ○   ○

---

10   **Which word has the same middle sound as <u>nine</u>?**

  six   rain   wild   find

   ○   ○   ○   ○

---

11   **Which word has the same middle sound as <u>fun</u>?**

  guess   great   jump   proud

   ○   ○   ○   ○

---

12   **Which word has the same middle sound as <u>pin</u>?**

  since   fast   stuff   soft

   ○   ○   ○   ○

GO

Directions: Find the word that means a small horse.

SAMPLE C

cow ○   kitten ○   chick ○   pony ○

13 **Find the word that means a color.**

chalk ○   paint ○   light ○   brown ○

14 **Find the word that means a tool.**

hammer ○   make ○   fix ○   wood ○

Directions: Find the answer that means about the same as the underlined word.

15 <u>speak</u> quietly

- ○ talk
- ○ play
- ○ study
- ○ walk

16 <u>muddy</u> car

- ○ fast
- ○ large
- ○ dirty
- ○ shiny

17 <u>remain</u> here

- ○ leave
- ○ play
- ○ eat
- ○ stay

18 <u>assist</u> them

- ○ call
- ○ help
- ○ join
- ○ like

GO

Directions: For Sample D and numbers 19–21, choose the word that fits best in the blank.

SAMPLE D Everybody left _____ me. I stayed and helped clean up.

- ○ and
- ○ beside
- ○ above
- ○ except

19 Each week, I try to save some money in my _____ .

- ○ pocket
- ○ wallet
- ○ bank

20 The _____ at the beach were pretty. I took some home.

- ○ shells
- ○ water
- ○ crowd

21 I _____ the table. This made the books fall off.

- ○ bumped
- ○ saw
- ○ drew
- ○ liked

Directions: For Sample E and numbers 22–25, solve the problems.

SAMPLE E

$$8 - 4$$

- ○ 12
- ○ 4
- ○ 48
- ○ 3

22

$$45¢ + 42¢$$

- ○ 96¢
- ○ 3¢
- ○ 87¢
- ○ 83¢

23

$$8 + 2$$

- ○ 10
- ○ 6
- ○ 11
- ○ 28

24

$$50 - 50$$

- ○ 10
- ○ 5
- ○ 0
- ○ 100

25

$$12 - 7 =$$

- ○ 4
- ○ 6
- ○ 19
- ○ 5

STOP

Mathematics

Directions: Which flag can be folded on the dotted line so the parts match?

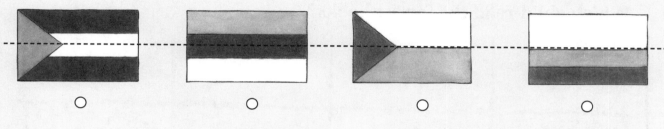

○   ○   ○   ○

1   **Which group has the largest number of nuts?**

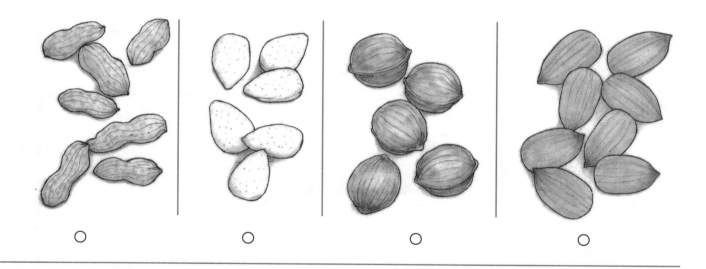

○   ○   ○   ○

2   **Which dress has both a triangle and a square on it?**

○   ○   ○   ○

GO

Name _____

THE BOOK CLUB

Sam, Mindy, Paul, and Sasha are members of the book club. The graph shows how many books they read this week. Use the graph to answer numbers 3 and 4.

3   **Which child read the fewest books?**

Sam	Mindy	Paul	Sasha
○	○	○	○

4   **Which children read the same number of books?**

Sam and Paul	Sam and Sasha	Sam and Mindy	Mindy and Sasha
○	○	○	○

GO

5 **Which child is counting by fours?**

12, 13, 14   20, 24, 28   12, 18, 24   15, 18, 21

○   ○   ○   ○

6 The pictures in the first row show how a piece of paper is folded and cut. **Find the shape that remains.**

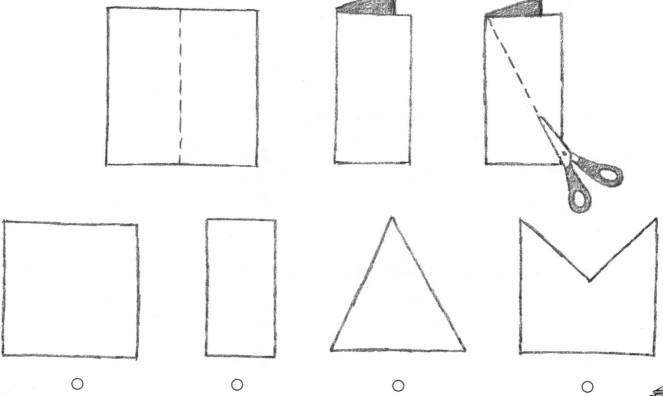

○   ○   ○   ○

GO

Saving Our Money

Directions: The table has tally marks that show the coins that Sam, Mindy, Paul, and Sasha have. Use this table to answer numbers 7 and 8.

	Sam	Mindy	Paul	Sasha
penny	||	|||	|	|||
nickel	||||/	|||	||	||||
dime	|||	|		
quarter		|	|||	||||

7 **Find the child who has the most coins.**

○   ○   ○   ○

8 **Find the child who has both a dime and a quarter.**

○   ○   ○   ○

STOP

Test Practice
Answer Key

This page intentionally left blank.

Grade 1 Record Your Scores

After you have completed and checked each test, record your scores below. Do not count your answers for the sample questions or the writing pages.

Practice Test

Unit 1 Reading and Language Arts
Number of Questions: 37   Number Correct _____

Unit 2 Basic Skills
Number of Questions: 62   Number Correct _____

Unit 3 Mathematics
Number of Questions: 15   Number Correct _____

Final Test

Unit 1 Reading and Language Arts
Number of Questions: 9   Number Correct _____

Unit 2 Basic Skills
Number of Questions: 25   Number Correct _____

Unit 3 Mathematics
Number of Questions: 8   Number Correct _____

Grade 1 Answer Key

Page 243

A. on the dish

B. The owl was on the turtle.

Page 244

1. the third picture

2. the first picture

3. She was sad.

4. fixing a bike

Page 245

5. strong

6. fly

7. line

8. ten

Page 247

9. He has long, brown hair.

10. by the door

11. bring it back.

Page 248

12. My Dog Nick

13. Is this Nick's ball?

14. He

Page 249

15. I wash the dog.

16. Then I drink some milk.

Page 250

A. kitten

B. pick

Page 251

1. the third picture

2. the first picture

3. the second picture

Page 252

4. the first picture

5. the third picture

6. the second picture

Page 253

7. leaf

8. gone

9. bag

10. rest

Grade 1 Answer Key

Page 254

Answers will vary, but the child should answer questions about the animal chosen, such as how it looks, where it lives, what it eats, and some of the things it does.

Page 255

Answers will vary, but the child should write how-to sentences about something he or she can do or make using four steps.

Page 256

A. eat
1. foot
2. second picture
3. third picture

Page 257

4. second picture
5. second picture
6. They were in the yard.
7. what a bird did

Page 258

8. comma
9. period
10. the coat
11. chris

Page 259

Paragraphs will vary but should describe the child's special day.

Page 260

A. boat
1. neat
2. desk
3. from
4. please
5. skip

Page 261

B. her
6. can
7. not
8. love
9. sent
10. heart

Grade 1 Answer Key

Page 262
- **C.** must
- **11.** need
- **12.** cake
- **13.** sock
- **14.** eat

Page 263
- **A.** large
- **1.** year
- **2.** orange
- **3.** house
- **4.** log
- **5.** bee

Page 264
- **B.** pick
- **C.** bad
- **6.** sleep
- **7.** fast
- **8.** under
- **9.** like
- **10.** stone
- **11.** clean

Page 265
- **D.** young
- **12.** start
- **13.** against
- **14.** dishes
- **15.** moon
- **16.** painted
- **17.** sharp

Page 266
- **A.** 5
- **1.** 10
- **2.** 7
- **3.** 40
- **B.** 4
- **4.** 6
- **5.** 61 cents
- **6.** 7

Page 267
- **A.** won
- **1.** fork
- **2.** more
- **3.** spill
- **4.** rug
- **5.** sled
- **6.** hold

Grade 1 Answer Key

Page 268
   B. heard
   7. round
   8. rest
   9. game
   10. root
   11. five
   12. hand

Page 269
   C. book
   13. town
   14. lake
   15. look
   16. ship
   17. hear
   18. damp

Page 270
   D. thin
   19. lift
   20. bake
   21. closet
   E. 12
   22. 72 cents
   23. 18
   24. 20 cents
   25. 58

Page 271
   A. second picture

Page 272
   1. 2

Page 273
   2. Grapes
   3. Bananas

Page 274
   4. the third circle
   5. the first picture

Page 275
   6. the third picture
   7. the glue

Page 276
   A. 10
   1. 36
   2. 16 cents

Page 277
   3. the second picture (ovals)
   4. the last picture

Grade 1 Answer Key

Page 278
  5. the last picture
  6. the last picture
  7. 5
  8. the second picture

Page 279
  A. a bee

Page 280
  1. Brenda looks sad.

Page 281
  2. He smiled at her.
  3. She was warm again.
  4. south
  5. They both fly.

Page 282
  6. lake
  7. boats
  8. them
  9. They flew to a warm place.

Page 283
Letters will vary, but the child should write a friendly letter.

Page 284
Stories will vary but should follow the story map.

Page 285
  A. jump
  1. pool
  2. vote
  3. choose
  4. club
  5. now
  6. hard

Page 286
  B. fort
  7. lock
  8. sink
  9. young
  10. find
  11. jump
  12. since

Grade 1 Answer Key

Page 287

C. pony
13. brown
14. hammer
15. talk
16. dirty
17. stay
18. help

Page 288

D. except
19. bank
20. shells
21. bumped
E. 4
22. 87 cents
23. 10
24. 0
25. 5

Page 289

A. first picture
1. last picture
2. last picture

Page 290

3. Paul
4. Mindy and Sasha

Page 291

5. second child
6. third picture

Page 292

7. last child
8. second child

This page intentionally left blank.

Test Practice
Worksheet

This page intentionally left blank.

Test Practice Worksheet

Test Practice Worksheet

Test Practice Worksheet

Test Practice Worksheet

Test Practice Worksheet

Test Practice Worksheet

Test Practice Worksheet

Test Practice Worksheet

Test Practice Worksheet

Test Practice Worksheet

Test Practice Worksheet

Test Practice Worksheet

Test Practice Worksheet

Test Practice Worksheet

Test Practice Worksheet

Test Practice Worksheet